When Your Lover Is a Liar

HEALING THE WOUNDS OF DECEPTION AND BETRAYAL

SUSAN FORWARD, Ph.D.,
with Donna Frazier

Quill

An Imprint of HarperCollins Publishers

ALSO BY SUSAN FORWARD:

Betrayal of Innocence
Men Who Hate Women and the Women Who Love Them
Toxic Parents
Obsessive Love
Money Demons
Emotional Blackmail

A hardcover edition of this book was published in 1999 by HarperCollins Publishers.

WHEN YOUR LOVER IS A LIAR. Copyright © 1999 by Susan Forward. All rights reserved. Printed in the United States of America. No part of this book may be used or reproduced in any manner whatsoever without written permission except in the case of brief quotations embodied in critical articles and reviews. For information address HarperCollins Publishers Inc., 10 East 53rd Street, New York, NY 10022.

HarperCollins books may be purchased for educational, business, or sales promotional use. For information please write: Special Markets Department, HarperCollins Publishers Inc., 10 East 53rd Street, New York, NY 10022.

First HarperPerennial edition published 2000.

Reprinted in Quill 2001.

Designed by Laura Lindgren

The Library of Congress has catalogued the hardcover editon as follows:

Forward, Susan
    When your lover is a liar: healing the wounds of deception and betrayal/Susan Forward.
    p. cm.
    ISBN 0–06–019142–2
    1. Men—United States—Sexual behavior. 2. Man-woman relationships—United States. 3. Women—United States—Psychology. 4. Men—United States—Psychology. 5. Intimacy (Psychology)—United States. I. Title.
HQ28.F67 1999
306.7—dc21   98–30851

ISBN 0-06-093115-9 (pbk.)

06 07 08 09 ❖/RRD 20 19 18 17

Contents

PART ONE

A Diagram of Deceit

1

The Labyrinth of Lying

- You answer the phone to hear a woman on the other end say, "Is this Betty? I thought it was time you knew that your husband and I have been seeing each other for the past two years. He doesn't love you. Why don't you just let him go?"
- You get a notice from the bank that a check you wrote has bounced. You indignantly call the bank, certain that you have eight or ten times that amount in the account you share with your husband. You're told you're overdrawn—and you know you didn't spend all the money.
- Your live-in lover swears he's stopped drinking and has been attending AA meetings regularly—and then you find a bottle of Scotch hidden in his tool chest.

Suddenly you've got vertigo. The world you thought you knew is spinning. Your mind races: Who is this person I thought I could trust? How many other lies have there been? You've been socked in the stomach. You don't know if you have a future with this man—and you wonder if you can believe anything he said in the past. All you know for certain is this: Your lover is a liar.

At this agonizing, bewildering time, finding a rational response is crucial—an important relationship hangs in the balance, and so does your own well-being. Yet no matter how alert we may be, most of us have no idea what steps to take when we encounter lies on this most intimate ground. Most of us don't have a clue about how to confront and counter the poison of a lover's lie. Faced with the disorientation of deception and betrayal, we tend to bounce between two extremes: we may deny and rationalize away our partner's behavior, or become so enraged we can't think. People who care about us may be yelling "Dump him!"—and we turn ballistic, losing our perspective in a fit of anger. Neither path brings us peace or lasting satisfaction.

All too often our lovers' lies leave us paralyzed. We find ourselves unable to make even the simplest decisions with our partners, because trust has disappeared, and we don't know when or if they are telling us the truth. We don't know what's real anymore, and we suffer terribly. A relationship with a liar can destroy our self-respect and our ability to trust our own perceptions and judgments. In the worst instances, an otherwise loving woman can become bitter, guarded, and walled-off, afraid to open her heart for fear of being betrayed again.

A friend of mine recently summed up the dilemma many a woman has faced: "I trusted my boyfriend more than I've ever trusted anyone," she told me, "and then I found out he was still sleeping with an old girlfriend while he was telling me he loved me. I'm afraid I can never trust another man again."

Lying by a lover is frequently one of the most destructive forces in a woman's life.

But it doesn't have to be.

There is a way through the labyrinth of lying in love relationships, and I'd like to give you a map to this subterranean world within a world. In the pages that follow, I will deal with the full range of lies, from the benign to the lethal, and introduce you to the many varieties of liars—from those who'd never admit what they're doing to the chronic confessors who encourage us to forgive and forget. I'll also give you a detailed profile of the one kind of liar you must leave immediately.

I will show you some of the forces that drive men to lie, how they behave, and how to stop them early on. In the second half of this book, I will give you specific communication skills and behavioral strategies that will go a long way toward helping you reground a relationship in honesty or, when that is not possible, decide when to leave a partner who lies. Whatever your situation, I will help you identify your best course of action, and I will support you through the process of bringing truth, self-trust, and intimacy back into your life.

A DIAGRAM OF DECEPTION

The words *lie* and *liar* are ugly. It's heartbreaking to have to use them to describe someone you love or are interested in, because they're loaded with pain and anger. They put you face-to-face with betrayal and malevolence when what you thought you had was intimacy. The words themselves are so inflammatory that it's important not to use them casually.

Certainly not every man is a liar, not every liar is a man, and not every thoughtless act is a lie. But in this book I'm focusing specifically on men who lie to women because I've seen how resistant women tend to be to acknowledging that the men they love lie to them. Women suffer uniquely when lies pop up in a relationship because, as we'll see, when a man lies to a woman, both of them blame her.

When I use the word *liar*, I'm not talking about men who mislead us inadvertently (because of oversights or misunderstandings) or with optimistic but unrealistic promises (like "I'll meet you at six" when they're not sure they can even get off work before seven).

And I'm not talking about the harmless little white lies that we all tell or shading the truth to protect a person from something painful. Most of us use flattery and exaggeration in our day-to-day interactions, and life could be pretty cruel if we didn't. The whole truth and nothing but the truth is fine in the courtroom, but we all try to soften otherwise harsh realities. We meet a friend we haven't seen in a few years and diplomatically say, "You look great—you haven't changed a bit," even as we're thinking, "God, you've got jowls just like your mother's, and the same bad taste in clothes." Do our words convey the whole truth? Of course not. But is a lie like this worth worrying about? I don't think so.

The lies that harm us and our relationships all involve an

intent to deceive. A lie is deliberate and conscious behavior that either misrepresents important facts or conceals and withholds them in order to keep you from knowing the truth about certain facets of your partner's past, present, and, often, future.

WHERE LYING THRIVES

When we hear words like *deception* and *betrayal*, we usually think of infidelity. And certainly every woman dreads finding out that her lover is cheating on her and is sexually involved with another woman. Discovering this kind of lie hits us where we are the most vulnerable. It attacks our very core and threatens our sense of safety and desirability. It both enrages and terrifies us, and it causes horrendous pain. Even in cases where the man insists that his action "didn't mean anything," an affair changes the relationship forever, and in some cases may end it.

But difficult as it may be for you to believe, other varieties of lies can equal or exceed affairs in the amount of havoc they wreak in your life. Lies are like dandelion seeds—they take root everywhere and flourish dangerously in every part of our lives. Throughout this book, you will get to know women whose lovers lie about money, addiction, commitment, availability, important events from their pasts, and the future. Often we dismiss these lies as inconsequential or even breathe a sigh of relief because "at least he's not having an affair." But as the women you will meet have discovered, a significant lie directed toward any aspect of your life can have a profound impact on your well-being.

THE TWO FACES OF LYING

Lies can be in what is said or in what is never mentioned. It's helpful to think of these two basic categories as lies of commission and lies of omission.

Lies of commission are blatant misstatements of fact about a man's life, behavior, and history, and they sound like this:

- "I am not having an affair" (when he is).
- "I made the house payment a week ago—the check must

have gotten lost in the mail" (when he hasn't mailed it).
- "I've been divorced for a year" (when he's still married).
- "I used to have a little problem with alcohol, but I've gotten over it" (when he's still drinking heavily).
- "I'm not seeing any other women" (when he is).
- "I'll never hit you again" (when he will).

IT'S JUST PLATONIC

My client Lee was deeply hurt by a lie of commission early in a relationship that she had high hopes for.

Lee is thirty-nine and divorced, and she works as an assistant manager in a men's clothing store in Los Angeles. She's originally from Central America and her lilting speech has a slight trace of an accent. Lee was flattered and intrigued when one of her steady customers, Barry, an attractive attorney in his late twenties, began flirting with her and then asked her out to dinner.

I told him right off the bat that I was older than him, and he said he'd always been with women in their thirties and forties because he found women his own age too immature and unsophisticated. Well, that was pretty reassuring. We started seeing each other—sometimes as much as two or three times a week. One night I was running late and I wanted to let him know, and I realized I didn't have his home phone—all I had was his pager number. When I asked him about it, he said that he had some roommates and that he didn't always get to answer his phone and he had some phone problems—and I should just use his pager number, something like that. It seemed a little too fishy to me and I said something, so he finally gave me his home phone.

Barry's runaround should have tipped Lee off. When you find that a new lover is ambiguous or evasive about such basics as where he lives, whom he lives with, whether he's married, and what his home phone number is, pay attention. This is vitally important behavioral information. If you ignore or overlook it, you may be in for some unpleasant shocks.

One night I called Barry to invite him to a party, and a girl answered. I hung up immediately. I felt really confused, and I asked him about it. He said yes, he lived with a girl, but she was just his roommate and that they'd been living together for three years. She was from another country—Guatemala, I think—and he was helping her out, but it was totally platonic. So I accepted that, and we kept seeing each other, and I'm getting more and more involved with him. He's pursuing me very hot and heavy and saying "I love you and I think we have a future together." But he never stayed the night. He would always have an excuse like "I have to get up really early in the morning—I have a lot of work to do." So I asked him why he couldn't stay over and he got real quiet and nervous, and then he told me that he couldn't do that to this girl. And I said, "What girl?" And he said, "Well, the girl I'm living with." So I asked him if they were a couple and he stammered a little bit, and finally he said yes.

It's easy, listening to Lee's story, to do some second-guessing. Surely she should have heard the warning bells and seen how protective Barry was being about the basic facts of his life. But Lee had done what many women do: projected her own character and values onto Barry. She assumed that since she was being honest with him, he was automatically being honest with her. When she questioned him, he first dodged her concerns, and then he lied to her by saying he lived with "some roommates." When she found this wasn't true, he lied further by misrepresenting a sexual relationship as a platonic one. Finally cornered, he continued the deception by turning up the romantic heat and assuring Lee that he really wanted to have a serious relationship with her, though he had no intention of breaking off with the other woman.

Lee's a confident, sophisticated woman—not stupid, not naive. But she wasn't looking for lies, she was looking for love. And with the temporary blinders of a hot new romance in place, she didn't recognize that the truth was eroding all around her.

THE RIGHT QUESTIONS, THE WRONG ANSWERS

When a man's lies of commission are part of a broad deception about the nature of his character, they can form a persuasive mirage that's hard to dispel, even when it's challenged by the truth. This is especially true when we've worked hard to protect ourselves by asking "all the right questions."

Kathy is a forty-five-year-old licensed vocational nurse who works on the children's ward at a large metropolitan hospital. She is a close friend of a colleague of mine, and when she heard I was working on this book, she got in touch with me and said she was eager to tell her story in the hope that it might help other women.

David and I met in a Twelve Step program through a mutual friend. In the program, it says you're not supposed to be in a relationship for a year while you're getting sober, so for a year David and I were just friends. No rushing things, just casual friends. When I hit my one year, we started going out. It started slow, but I became very attracted to him. We had the same interests—music, cats, books—the same sense of humor, and we had a lot of the same values. We both wanted a close big family, even though neither of us wanted children. But we were very involved with our nieces and nephews and other members of our families. We had a deep respect for each other's need to be sober. Believe me, I was watching him and listening to him and asking his friends about him—doing everything I could to be sure he wasn't going to be another guy with problems or a wife on the side, something like that. I'm not as easy to fool as I used to be.

Four months after we started dating, he cut his hand very badly at work, and I moved in with him to take care of him because he couldn't do much for himself. I never moved out. I know it was quick, but then again, it wasn't. We had spent all that time slowly getting to know each other.

I was careful, too. We talked a lot about money because I made quite a bit more than he did and I wanted to be sure that it wasn't going to be a problem—and I wanted to get some sense of how he handled his finances. He told me he'd never bounced a

*check, he kept a real tight budget, and he had no debts except his
car payments. When he wanted something he would save for it.
That impressed the hell out of me.*

Kathy did all the right things. She knew David as a friend
before they started dating, she didn't rush into marriage, and she
asked direct questions, listening for honest answers. She made
sure that she and David talked about their expectations and values about children, finances, and sobriety. She felt safe and confident—a feeling that continued even when she saw evidence to
the contrary.

*One day, a few weeks after we started living together, I got
the mail and saw an IRS notice. It turned out that he hadn't
filed his taxes for three years and he owed them thirteen thousand dollars. Oh sure, I was concerned, but he had good answers
for everything I brought up. He said he'd already taken steps to
deal with the debt—he said it was from his old drinking days—
and he assured me that he and the IRS had agreed on a repay-
ment plan.*

Kathy smoothed over a major lie on David's part. Not filing
taxes is serious business, and if David were really as financially
responsible as she wanted to believe he was, he would not have a
$13,000 tax debt. As it was, she soon discovered, he had no plan
at all for repaying the money. But faced with the gap between her
glowing perception of David and the more troubling reality,
Kathy held on to her original perception. She felt she could trust
him—after all, he'd been so "open," it was inconceivable to her
that everything he'd said about his financial status was fabri-
cated.

Could Kathy have known? Should she have realized that
David was not the poster boy for financial responsibility? Oh
sure, she could have run credit checks on him or asked him
about any debts that might come back to haunt her were she to
marry him—and I'm not saying a woman should never do that.
But how many of us are willing to turn into a private detective in
the early stages of a relationship, especially when we've been

given no reason to be suspicious? Love and suspicion seem so contradictory. David said all the right things, seemed to be doing all the right things, and he attended meetings regularly—but as with all men who lie, he was in charge of what Kathy got to know and didn't get to know, and he wanted to keep it that way. As a result, the truth and their relationship began to decay. The missed tax payments were only the beginning. There was a lot more active lying that Kathy didn't discover until they were married and she was deeply involved with him and his family.

WHAT YOU DON'T KNOW WILL HURT YOU

Lies of omission are justified by the old saw "What you don't know won't hurt you." Using evasion and secrecy, your lover withholds information that he knows would make you feel hurt or angry or even cause you to end the relationship. Concealment allows him to do whatever he wants and keep you in the dark.

One of my favorite examples of this kind of lying is an exchange that took place between a friend of mine, Beth, and her live-in lover, Roger. Beth had been suspicious for some time that Roger was cooling toward her. He had started coming home later and later, and there were frequent phone calls whispered behind closed doors. So she decided to confront him directly. "I asked him if he was having an affair, and he answered with complete seriousness, 'Nobody said that yet.' What the hell is that supposed to mean? Is that a yes? Is that a no? If it isn't said, then it can't be happening, so I can't accuse him of lying to me?"

I can't give you an example of how lies of omission sound because they fall silently into the spaces between words. But they usually involve neglecting to tell you such "little" things as:

- "I'm having an affair."
- "I'm living with another woman."
- "I have a child in another state."
- "I'm bisexual."
- "I'm an alcoholic/drug user/compulsive gambler."
- "I'm manic-depressive and there's a long history of mental illness in my family" (or any other significant mental or physical problem).

- "I have herpes/am HIV-positive."
- "I'm on probation/have a criminal record."
- "I'm in debt/I have money problems/I'm unstable financially."

THE MOST COMMON LIE OF OMISSION

While some men who are having affairs voluntarily confess when the combined pressure of lying and guilt become intolerable for them, most don't. Instead, their relationship with another woman (or women) remains secret as long as they can keep the deception going. However, this particular lie of omission is almost always discovered, often in a way that is cruel and humiliating for the man's partner.

My client Anne, forty-seven, is a gentle and ethereal-looking woman who has just recently returned to school to get her master's in education. Her husband of fifteen years, Randy, is an executive in a video company that does educational and documentary films. They have one child, Samantha, whom they both adore. Anne's life was happy and fulfilling until one morning about two weeks before she came to see me for the first time:

I got the mail when I came home from school, as I usually do, but there was nothing usual about that day. There was a letter addressed to me on Randy's company letterhead, which was pretty strange. I opened it and my whole world came crashing down. The letter was from someone in the office—it wasn't signed. It said, "We really like you and think you should know that Randy is involved with a woman in the office and she's going to be meeting him on the trip he's taking to Chicago."

I barely remember what the rest of it said—I felt so physically sick. I called him at work and he actually admitted it right away and said he was coming right home. We've been trying to get through this on our own, but I'm just crying all the time—I can't deal with anything.

Men who are involved with other women appear, as ridiculous as it may seem, to genuinely believe that they won't get caught, even when friends or business associates are aware of what's going on. From Randy's point of view, he had everything to lose and little to gain if he didn't keep his lies of omission going. But in Randy's case, somebody else made the decision for him. And once his lies of omission came to light, his marriage would never be the same.

WHEN THE PAST IS A LIE

Anne found out about Randy's affair from a third party, a scenario that many women are familiar with. In fact, most lies of omission, whatever they're about, are discovered in just that way.

In my first meeting with Jan, she told me how she had come face-to-face with a whopper of a lie of omission a few days before she was supposed to get married.

Jan was thirty-six and had a successful graphic design business at the time she met Bill, a dynamic and charming mortgage broker, on a date arranged by mutual friends. The chemistry between them was instant and intense, and after just a few months, they decided to get married. Then the roof fell in.

One morning, shortly before their scheduled wedding, Jan got some information that could have changed everything.

We'd both been married before and had five kids between us. His children were with his ex-wife and my two were with us. We knew there would be a lot of adjustments to make and a lot of things to work through, but we were truly in love and I was ecstatically happy.

He was moving the last of his things from his apartment into my house, and he had gone over there early to meet the movers. I was in that delicious place between being asleep and just starting to wake up when the phone rang.

It was a woman. She said, "Is this Jan?" I said it was, and then she said, "You don't know me, but maybe you've heard my name. I'm Carla, Bill's second ex-wife." I wasn't fully awake yet, and my first thought was that somebody was pulling some kind of joke, because Bill was still close to a lot of his old college fraternity pals and they were always kidding around and acting pretty adolescent when they got together. But there was something in her voice—something almost menacing—that told me this was no joke. I asked her what she wanted and she said she wanted to talk to Bill and assumed he'd be at my place. I mumbled something about him not being there . . . and hung up. Needless to say, I was in a daze. What the hell was going on?

He came in about an hour later, and I just pounced on him. I bombarded him with questions. Had he really been married twice and just neglected to tell me about it? Didn't he know me well enough to know it wouldn't have made any difference? Why did he think he had to lie to me? Didn't he trust me? And what else had he lied about?

Jan's anger was justified, as was her mistrust. But as we'll see, Jan's first glimpse of the truth was quickly obscured by Bill's explanations and her need to believe them. Lies like Bill's are powerful because it's easy for a man to use the charm and promises of the present to overshadow the troubling images that seem to be receding in the rearview mirror.

A "SMALL OVERSIGHT"

Carol, a legal secretary, was a client of mine several years ago. She had been in a difficult, lie-filled marriage for more than twenty years, married to a man who was a master of withholding vital information about his life from her. Some men expose their pasts to us stintingly, at best, though they may often seem forthcoming, and what they don't tell you about their lives could fill a library.

I thought Ken was cute, and he had a pretty good job as a mechanic. He really came on strong, and after three weeks of dating, I married him. I was on the rebound, and I wanted to spite my old boyfriend and my parents, who didn't approve of Ken at all. I really knew nothing about him, but it didn't seem to matter.

I was working for a bank, and I got a wonderful opportunity to take a job at a company that did aerial photography for the government. It was real classified stuff, so they wanted me to get a security clearance, which was no problem as far as I was concerned.

On the clearance form, there was a question that asked if your spouse had ever been convicted of a misdemeanor or a felony, so I asked Ken about it. He said, "I got a few traffic tickets but that's all." So that's what I put on the application.

They hired me and I was on a thirty-day trial period while they were doing my security clearance. I loved it. Here I am twenty-four years old and I have my own office and a really fascinating job. Then one day, about two weeks after I started, my boss called me in and said there were two "agents" who wanted to see me. I went into my boss's office and one of the investigators said, "Mrs. Adams, why did you lie on your application?" When I told them I didn't know what they meant, one of them said, "Your husband is currently on probation for a felony. I suggest you talk it over with him. It involves a drug charge."

Ken's lie of omission cost Carol the job she loved, and of course her first impulse was to leave him. But jobless, newly pregnant, and afraid to admit her difficulties to her disdainful parents, she decided to stick it out, wanting to believe the worst was over. As often happens, though, Ken's lie had undermined some important foundations of her life—her job and reputation, to name two—and left her vulnerable to the years of lies that were yet to come.

A man can slip easily into a lie about the past because the past is already hidden. Withholding information that might be troubling is easier than revealing it, and there's a natural tendency to wait until you've established rapport with someone before testing their trust with a difficult disclosure. Besides, the rationalization goes, the past is the past. What matters, he tells himself—and you, if you find out—is that he's treating you well, he loves you, and he's grown up and reformed since his wild old days, or he's gotten past old troubles. Therefore, what he's not telling you is none of your business—even when it costs you what you value most.

HE CONTROLS WHAT YOU KNOW

Whatever prompts the lie—whether it's a lie of omission or one of commission—whatever a man's particular style of lying may be, and whatever he lies about, certain facts will always be constant:

- He becomes the sole proprietor of the truth.
- He is the only one who knows what's really going on, so he has control and power over the events of your life.
- You don't get to know information that can drastically affect you.
- You can't make an informed choice about major life decisions, such as, Should I marry this man? Should I stay with him? Do I need to take certain steps to protect myself emotionally or financially?
- You don't know who he really is.

His lies keep you completely in the dark—locked in a fool's paradise.

TRUTH DECAY

How did the relationship erode from point A—"He's a great guy"—to point B—"I'm involved with a liar"? Sometimes, as in Lee's case, there are telltale signs along the way, and sometimes, as with Jan, there are no clues at all to what's coming. Men who lie to us don't wear signs, and some of the worst liars even lie to themselves about their behavior. Since none of us has a crystal ball, there is often no way to predict whether the man you love or are interested in will turn out to be an honorable guy, an occasional liar, or a chronic one. Just about everyone looks good in the beginning, and trying to figure out what's real and what's a facade without any solid information is a waste of time and energy.

It takes time for someone's true character to emerge, and when it does, it may be very different from what you thought it was.

IS IT A LIE OR ISN'T IT?

There's some small comfort in being able to see clearly what's happening, even if it's the discovery that your lover is a liar. That's black-and-white. It's tangible, and you have something to deal with. But not every misrepresentation or withholding of truth is as clear and unambiguous as the ones we've seen so far. And we can make ourselves crazy asking "What just happened? Was it a lie or just a bad case of crossed wires and miscommunication?" The defining characteristic of a lie is its intent to deceive, but sometimes intent is murky. This is often true in the early stages of a relationship.

THE DATING GAME

When we're being romanced, we don't want to be deceived about anything important, but we love to hear things like "You're the most beautiful woman I've ever been with" and "I've never been as excited about any woman as I am about you," even though we know those statements may not be completely true. We understand that such words are designed to win us in the ritual of courtship and seduction.

We all enjoy having our egos stroked, and while a relationship is still at an early stage, the fact that we're both playing a few games with the truth doesn't make too much difference. We know that our potential partner will often exaggerate and preen to build himself up in our eyes. And we're usually doing the same thing.

The hazards arise when a man maintains the facades of courtship as a relationship deepens and uses them to catch us up in unrealistic expectations and hopes.

THE DISAPPEARING LOVER

My friend Nina, a forty-eight-year-old paralegal, found herself facing a situation all too common for a lot of women—the mystery of the disappearing lover.

I saw Tom almost every night for a month, and one night we were sitting watching a romantic movie on television when he took my hand and told me, "I want an exclusive relationship with you. I don't want to see anyone else, and I hope you don't want to see anyone else either." My heart was pounding, and I was thrilled.

He said he had to go to Denver on business, and he'd be back on the weekend and call me every day from the road. He didn't call once, and I didn't know how to reach him. The weekend came and I still didn't hear from him. So I finally called him at home. He was very cool, very evasive. He said he was exhausted and really didn't have a chance to call me while he was gone. I was panicked, but I tried not to show it. He sounded like a totally different person—like a stranger.

I asked him when I was going to see him, and he mumbled something about how he thought we ought to cool it for a while—that things were moving too fast for him! This was the same guy who just six days before had asked for an exclusive relationship! Now I'm left with all these unanswered questions. Did I do something to scare him or drive him away? What was going on with him? Was any of it real?

MISSING IN ACTION

Anyone who's ever been involved in a hot-one-minute-cold-the-next relationship knows how bewildering and disorienting it can be. We replay conversations in our minds and ask what we did to scare him off. We're crushed to find that something we thought was wonderful and had potential for the future was an illusion. But was Tom a liar? Did he intend to deceive Nina? While I can't get inside Tom's head, I have a strong hunch that he was a guy who may have meant what he said in the heat of the moment but scared himself to death with too much too soon and didn't have the courage or the tools to express his ambivalence and change of heart. Maybe he was commitment-phobic and trying to convince himself that he wasn't afraid of an intimate relationship; maybe he'd had terrible experiences with women in the past; maybe he hates his mother—we'll never know.

But one thing is certain: instead of talking out his fears and conflicts or embarrassment about having led Nina on, he acted them out by withdrawing abruptly. Tom was probably far less emotionally available than he portrayed himself to be, but it's not clear he knew that until he realized he was in over his head with Nina. I think Tom, like many men, is less than fluent in the language of feelings. It's a cliché that men have a tough time knowing and expressing what they feel—but that doesn't keep it from being true of many men, who often look as if they're lying because of it. I'd bet that Tom got overwhelmed with feelings he didn't know how to deal with in a situation that got out of hand, and he took what was for him the easy way out. Looks like a lie, sounds like a lie, hurts like a lie—but it's probably not.

SOMETIMES HE'LL SAY ANYTHING

The issue of intent is a tricky one. We can't climb inside our lover's mind and look into a corner labeled "Intent" to see if something he told us at one time was actually a lie when it turns out, down the line, not to be true.

When a man deliberately misstates or withholds important facts, his intent is obviously deceptive. But some men, like Tom, say things they truly mean at the time and under circumstances that exist in that moment, only to change their minds later. These changes of heart or mind may involve such major life issues as:

- Whether or not he intends to marry you
- Whether or not he wants children
- What his sexual needs and preferences are
- Who should work and how finances will be divided
- Where you will be living
- How much involvement with members of his family you will be expected to have

If he reverses himself on issues as significant as these, it's only natural to cry foul and accuse him of having lied to you at the time he told you what you wanted to hear. But did he really lie to you, or did he just fail to think things through? Certainly he may have been thoughtless, impulsive, and maybe even out of touch with what he really felt and wanted when he made certain representations to you. But if he had no deliberate intent to deceive you, he's not a liar.

On the other hand, some men know at the time that they have no intention of following through on what they're telling you.

Paula had met John in high school. They'd been great friends, but lost touch with each other after graduation. Then, when they were in their twenties, they met again at a school reunion, and the romance began.

We were moving toward a sexual relationship, and I told John I had something very painful to tell him and I was scared how he might react. He told me, "You can trust me with anything—I love you." I felt so safe with him, so I told him about how I got raped when I was thirteen. I was walking home from school through this field when this guy jumped me and pulled a knife on me. I thought I was going to die. He made me do oral sex on him. I'd never even seen a man's thing before—I was just a kid. It was horrible and repulsive. I told John that I didn't think I could do that with a man, and he promised he would never ask me to do anything that was unpleasant for me. We got married about three months later and I was in heaven. I really adored this man, and I thought our sex life was pretty good.

A couple of months into the marriage we were fooling around and he pulled my head down toward his genitals and I freaked: "I can't do this. I told you that." But he kept coaxing me. He told me I had to get over this—I think it became a challenge to him. When I said, "What about your promise?" he said, "That's not a promise you can expect any man to keep."

John had made a promise he knew he would break. He assured Paula that he would be understanding, but when his wishes were denied, he became coercive instead.

Like many men who lie, he was willing to say almost anything his partner wanted to hear in order to close the deal, figuring that he'd handle the problem later.

A classic example of a man who is deceiving you by promising something he knows he won't make good on is the married man who keeps you in a relationship with him by painting a glowing picture of the future you will have together, knowing he has no intention of leaving his wife. That is a lie. He knows it, and it's only a matter of time before you know it too.

SECRETS AND LIES

Let's wade a little further into the behavior we can't quite pin down as lying but that causes us a lot of confusion. What about secrets? All lies involve secrets, after all, but not all secrets are lies. I know those can be fighting words in the wars of truth between men and women. Women prize openness, connection, intimacy. Men want a little space, and often resent having to be accountable to anyone. Sometimes these conflicting needs can create situations in which men look to us as though they're lying and sneaking around, even when they're really not.

My friend Michael expressed this frustration, which I've heard from a number of men through the years:

We've actually got a great marriage, as you know, and I really love Joni, but she's got this one quirk that drives me nuts. She insists that I tell her about everything that's happened during the day—and what I thought and felt, and everything I think and feel about her . . . and it's wearing me out. I feel like I did when I was a little kid and my mother would interrogate me. I just don't spend as much time in the world of feelings as she does, or wants me to. I don't want to have a therapy session when I come home, and when I tell her that, she says I must have something to hide!

THE MYTH OF TELLING EACH OTHER EVERYTHING

Some women believe that in an ideal healthy relationship there are no secrets. Everything is out in the open. Every thought, every feeling, every action is shared, talked out, explored, and processed as it comes up. And if that doesn't happen, they believe there's something dark and even duplicitous going on.

That's why it's important to establish some ground rules about what partners have a right to know and what they have a right to keep to themselves. I would suggest that the following issues should be clarified between you.

If you are in a serious relationship or marriage, you have a right to know about:

1. Infidelity
2. How much money he makes, investment plans and goals, how his will is set up
3. All major financial information including bankruptcies, credit problems, significant financial problems, and debts
4. His past history of marriage, children, and divorce
5. Physical or psychological conditions that affect him or members of his immediate family that could have an impact on you or children you have or plan to have

Let me give you an example of why this last issue is so important. I once dated a wonderful man I'll call Jim. As our relationship deepened, we were both aware that there was a possibility we'd have a future together. I knew very little about his family, and he seldom talked about it. I had met his father and stepmother, and they seemed like lovely people. I'd once asked him if he had any sisters or brothers. He told me that he had had a sister, but "she died." I told him I was sorry and asked about how she died. His answer was vague—something about an incurable illness.

I accepted his answer—I had no reason not to. But several weeks later at a small dinner party, I was seated next to his business partner. We got on the subject of families, and he mentioned something about Jim's sister having committed suicide. I told him I hadn't known about that, and he became very upset—he'd assumed that since Jim and I were so close, I must have known.

I would like to think that Jim would have told me on his own, especially if we were contemplating marriage. If there was a genetic predisposition to depression in his family, I certainly had the right to know.

There are some secrets, often involving what your lover perceives as a shameful event in his family, that out of loyalty to them, he keeps secret from you but that involve information you need in order to make a fully informed choice about your relationship.

Your lover does not have the right to put loyalty to his family ahead of your right to make an informed choice when it involves dangerous secrets like alcoholism, child abuse, depression, suicide, violent behavior, or serious physical or mental illnesses. For example, you would certainly think twice about marrying a man whose father was a wife beater and a child abuser until you had some assurance that your lover had done some personal work on the psychological problems that inevitably stem from these experiences and are often handed down through the generations.

This does not mean your lover must open up his entire life to your scrutiny.

I strongly believe he has a right to:

1. Have private fantasies (including sexual ones), dreams, and daydreams
2. Keep some of his thoughts and feelings to himself
3. Enjoy unaccounted-for time
4. Keep some of his business and financial problems to himself, as long as they're temporary and he's working them out
5. Not tell you about every female colleague or friend he has lunch or a drink with

I know it's not easy for any woman to accept that her lover has corners of his life and mind that don't include her, but this kind of acceptance is an essential part of the delicate balance between having a life and sharing one. Your partner is not you. He has his own inner world, beliefs, and values. Keeping parts of his life to himself is not lying. Remember: Secrets become lies only when they involve a deliberate intent to deceive.

Once you realize that your lover is a liar, you can see that you've been living in parallel realities. There's the known world of the man you trust, and there's the world you've only glimpsed of a man who is working to keep his real life and intentions hidden. It seems almost impossible to reconcile the fact that the great guy you love is the same person who's been lying to you. But once the realities intersect, you begin to see the whole complex picture. And the decisions you make about how you will travel through this multilayered world will determine what happens to the relationship—and to your life.

2

The Manipulations That
Keep Us Hooked

We don't have a chance of holding our own against a man who is lying to us, and we can't put an end to the lying until we understand what he's doing and how he's doing it. Only then can we begin to recognize his manipulations and find effective ways of responding to them. It's difficult, though, because there's no one way of keeping the cycle of lies going. In fact, I've identified a vast and creative array of techniques used by liars when they fear that they'll be found out, or once their lies are discovered. Every one of them is designed to keep us from seeing the lie for what it is, crying foul, and taking action.

In some instances, these techniques are calculated and deliberate. In others, your lover may not even be aware of how manipulative he's being. But whatever approach he uses, it will tap one of two powerful forces—denial or confession. His goal: to get you to accept his explanations, believe them, back off, end the confrontation, and go back to the status quo.

DENIAL: IT NEVER HAPPENED

"Who, me?"
"I would never do such a thing."
"Are you crazy?"

Confronted with your evidence or suspicions, many men will take what seems like the most direct route to defending themselves: deny everything. Denying is a natural response to being caught as children, and it can be disarming coming from the little boy with his hand in the cookie jar who's telling you he's not the one who's been sneaking treats. Strange as it seems, it can also be absolutely persuasive coming from the men we love. You might be holding a love letter he wrote to his mistress or a copy of a statement showing huge losses from a bad investment he said he wouldn't make, but he can often transform even the most damning evidence with variations on the deny-it defense.

TECHNIQUE NO. 1: JUST SAY NO

- "No, I didn't."
- "No, I have no idea what that note is about."
- "No, I didn't take the money out of the bank."

When he believes he has a great deal of credibility with you, when you've backed him into a corner and a direct response is required, or when he's feeling cocky and confident, a man who lies, when confronted with your concerns, may just say no. Nothing complicated or elaborate here—just a simple no in response to whatever question you raise about his behavior. Question: "Are you having an affair?" "Did you lend your brother money?" "Were you out gambling?" Answer: A firm, clear "No, I'm not!" "No, I didn't!" "No, I wasn't!"

Straight denial was the response of choice when Jan, the graphic designer, confronted her husband-to-be, Bill, with the call from a woman who'd said she was his ex-wife:

He said that Carla was a real nut case and had delusions of marrying him, but I shouldn't pay any attention to it, she was trying to make trouble between us. I pleaded with him to just tell me the truth. I told him I could handle anything as long as he didn't lie to me, but he stuck to his story. I know it sounds ridiculous, but I believed him. He looked me straight in the eye,

*told me he loved me, and said that if I loved him I would know
he was telling the truth. I felt guilty for even asking.*

If you don't believe his no, and he sees that he hasn't managed to placate you and gotten you to stop interrogating him, he
will move on to a variety of other techniques, elaborating on his
original denial.

TECHNIQUE NO. 2: THE BEST DEFENSE IS A GOOD OFFENSE

Many liars face down confrontations with righteous indignation.
They make a fuss and divert attention from the subject at hand
by going on the offensive. This technique has several advantages:
he doesn't have to make excuses, scramble to cover himself, or
lie about the lie. Instead he can do what politicians and bureau-
crats have often done when caught: issue a denial and intimidate
the accuser into backing down.

My client Nora, a teacher in her late twenties, faced her husband's righteous indignation when she stumbled onto evidence
that Allen might be seeing another woman. Nora had never
thought of her marriage as ideal, but she thought she and Allen, a
thirty-five-year-old veterinarian, were working to iron out the differences that come up in any relationship. That all changed one
midsummer afternoon.

*I wanted to get a credit card for a phone order, so I picked
up his wallet. I wasn't snooping—I didn't think I had any reason to snoop. But I saw a piece of paper with two initials, CG,
and a phone number. At the time I didn't think too much about
it, but later I asked him, "Who's CG?" He just exploded and
said, "What are you doing looking in my wallet? You have no
business snooping around in my things. What are you going to
do next, start spying on me? What's gotten into you, anyway?"
I didn't push it because I just didn't want to set him off
again. And I did feel kind of guilty for going through his wallet, even though it was totally innocent. I ended up apologiz-
ing to him.*

Men like Allen can, if they're volcanic enough in their responses, shut down our ability and desire to question or confront them. In Allen's case, anger at Nora also served as a convenient excuse for becoming more secretive in their daily life. Nora began to notice that Allen no longer left his wallet or calendar lying around, and she blamed herself for driving a wedge between them when he retreated to the den to take phone calls or snatched pieces of mail out of her hands.

For a time at least, Allen succeeded in eliminating both confrontation and conversation about Nora's suspicions—she stopped asking and kept her doubts to herself until she no longer could.

A Word of Warning

If you are with a man who has a propensity for violence or who you suspect might cross the line from verbal to physical intimidation, confronting him with his lying could be very dangerous for you. Losing face or being made to look bad is often all it takes to set off a man who acts out his anger through physical assault. Of course, you shouldn't be with a man like this to begin with, but I'm enough of a realist to acknowledge that millions of women are. In the second half of this book, I will help you find the best course of action if you are in this kind of relationship.

TECHNIQUE NO. 3: THE POOR BABY

- "I'm so hurt you could doubt me."
- "I thought we trusted each other."
- "How could you think I would do such a thing?"

Spoken with a catch in his voice and perhaps a mist of tears in his eyes, phrases like these are intended to shift your attention from the liar to the lover. You may know him, now, to be a person who has hurt you and betrayed your trust, but he'd like to remind you of the man you fell in love with, the sensitive, vulnerable guy who has always loved you.

My client Diane, who does paralegal work, faced the confusion of her husband's poor-baby approach shortly after Ben's single daughter became pregnant at twenty-one:

Peggy moved up from San Diego to be near us, and that was great because we both wanted to be supportive, and we wanted to be there for her. The thing that shocked me, both before and after the baby was born, was that Peggy acted as though she was incapable of doing anything for herself. She seemed to think that Ben should take care of her. Once the baby was born, she was healthy and perfectly capable of working—my sister even found her a nice job in a day-care center, where she could have been with the baby—but all she wanted to do was sit in her apartment and watch TV.

Ben is always running over to give her money and buy her things, and it really has a huge impact on our finances. I plead with him not to give her any money—he's just helping her stay dependent and irresponsible by doing it. Ben looks like he's listening to me, and he assures me he'll stop indulging Peggy. But then she calls and he's out the door again. The last time this happened, I asked him what was going on, and he was pretty evasive.

I said, "Just please tell me the truth." And he looked very hurt and put his arms around me and said, "I am telling the truth. I need to see my daughter and the baby, but I'm not giving her money, because I know we can't afford it. You know I would never lie to you. Whatever happened to trust?" I felt terrible for doubting him—he's really a great guy.

There's no anger here, and no hint of menace, just a neat reversal of the situation. He's not the one hurting you with lies. You're the one who's hurting him by letting your suspicions overshadow all the good things between you. The upset between you is causing him great pain—and you end up feeling guilty.

TECHNIQUE NO. 4: ACCUSE SOMEONE ELSE OF LYING

- "Your friend is just trying to break us up by saying she saw me with someone else. She's never liked me and she's lying."
- "How can you believe my brother and not me?"
- "Your sister is such an unhappy woman she's lying about me because she envies our relationship."

When you confront your lover with evidence of a lie that you got from someone else, he may very well tell you that if there's lying involved, he's not the one who's doing it. According to him, the other person has something to gain by making him look bad. There's no one at fault here except the bearer of the bad news.

My client Allison, a thirty-eight-year-old photographer, had faced a lot of family opposition when she married Scott, an entrepreneur. Her parents, and especially her sister, Erica, had found him to be too slick and thought he was a phony from the beginning. When they tried to express their concerns to Allison, she wouldn't listen to any of it. But one afternoon she got a phone call from her sister that was very disturbing:

Scott had this old college friend Keith, who was a total screw-up. Scott was always bailing him out of jail for drunk driving or lending him money. All this guy had to do was call, and Scott would rush over to help him. One evening Scott got a phone call and told me that he had to go over to the Beverly Hills jail and bail Keith out. I asked him why he didn't just let Keith handle his own problems for once, and he said he couldn't do that to an old buddy. I went to sleep around eleven, but I don't sleep well when he's not there, so I tossed and turned. I heard him come in about three. I never thought anything about it.

The next day my sister called me at work. She said, "Look, I struggled all morning with whether I should tell you this, but I decided I have to. If you get mad at me, so be it, but you've got to know the truth. I was at the Beverly Hills Hotel last night, and Scott was there having a drink at the bar and being very affectionate with some blond I've never seen before. He didn't see me, but they left together. Sweetie, it's killing me to have to tell you, but I think this guy's a real SOB."

Naturally, I was devastated, but I told myself there was probably a logical explanation for it. We had such an intense, exciting relationship, I couldn't believe he could want or need anybody else.

Allison's first reaction to her sister's news was a combination of disbelief and panic. The world was turned upside down for her, and the only way to right it again was to go to the source—Scott. The problem was, Scott was a skilled manipulator, and extremely persuasive in shifting responsibility for his lies to other people.

I told Scott about Erica's call, and he got really angry. He said, "Your sister is some piece of work. First she tries to talk you out of marrying me, and now she's trying to wreck what we have. You know exactly where I was last night—I was getting Keith out of jail. She must have seen someone who looked like me." When I asked him why he got home so late, he said he had to wait a long time while they did the paperwork, and then he took Keith home and stayed to talk to him. He said he was trying to persuade Keith to join AA and just lost sight of the time. He's such a loyal friend to his buddies that it all sounded believable. Of course, I could have checked out his story, but I didn't want to. I didn't want to look like I was spying on him. So I believed him—and that made my sister a liar.

Allison is a prime example of how much women want to believe their lovers and how much energy we put into protecting the men in our lives at the expense of our own well-being and our relationships with other people who care about us. She could have checked with the police to see if Keith had indeed been arrested, or asked Keith himself, although men who lie often enlist someone to cover for them. But like so many women, Allison believed that any effort to find out the truth would reflect badly on her image of herself as a loving, trusting woman.

The technique of accusing someone else shifts your attention from "Did he lie to me?" to "Where are my loyalties?" And often we choose loyalty to our lovers over a protective concern for ourselves.

Shifting the Blame to a Child

It's bad enough when your lover accuses another adult of lying or telling you stories because, according to him, they have an axe to grind. But the technique is particularly insidious when it involves blaming children. When your lover tells you one story and your child another, you find yourself torn between the most important people in your life.

Early in their marriage, Carol's husband, Ken, had cost her a wonderful job by lying about his past. But Carol was convinced she could straighten Ken out, even as he became increasingly difficult to live with. Over time he became verbally abusive, drinking quite a bit and often staying out until early in the morning. Still, Carol hung in there:

I know I should have left him many times, but I felt so trapped with my kids, and I was afraid of what a divorce would do to my family. The last straw came when Ken took our youngest son, Jeff, on a camping trip and ended up leaving him in a motel overnight. Jeff told me about it when they got back, and when I asked Ken what in the world he was thinking of to leave a little boy alone like that, he said that Jeff was lying! He said kids always make up stories to get attention, and I'd better get my priorities straight and figure out where my loyalties should be.

Children are easy targets in these situations because men know how hard it is for a child to have credibility against an adult. An irresponsible parent like Ken has nothing to gain and a great deal to lose, from his point of view, if he is found out and acknowledges his behavior. What better way to deny his actions than by accusing the child of lying or making up stories?

Fortunately, Carol believed her son. If she hadn't, she would have betrayed him and her role as a mother and protector, just as surely as Ken had betrayed her and their son with his lies. Sadly, some women, when faced with this choice, do just that.

TECHNIQUE NO. 5: CREATIVE FICTION (BEGINNING CLASS)

When it's not convenient or comfortable to simply deny a transgression, some men opt for a most creative approach: they make up stories. The cover-up doesn't have to be elaborate. Some men stick to the plausible, piling one explanation on the next every time their partner unearths another aspect of the lie. The strategy here is never to admit the truth but to keep the lying game alive by answering every question or accusation with an excuse. Keep her focused on the investigation, looking for the indisputable "smoking gun," rather than stopping to assess the relationship and whether she wants it.

As Nora focused more on finding evidence of her husband's affair with CG, her husband dropped his direct denials and began countering her questions with invented explanations:

Things would be OK for a couple of days, and then he started coming home late. I knew he wasn't a drinker, so he wasn't at a bar. But he always had a story. He had to see a client after work—which didn't make sense because he did the sort of work where you don't see customers after business hours. He was a lousy liar, but that didn't seem to matter to him.

Then I found a cigarette butt with lipstick on it in the ashtray of the car, though neither of us smoked. When I questioned him, he first got very angry and then started weaving and dodging: "Oh yeah—I remember now. I had to give so-and-so a ride because her car was in the shop." Always an answer, always a story.

TECHNIQUE NO. 6: CREATIVE FICTION (MASTER CLASS)

Some men make up stories that are so wild we convince ourselves they must be true, even as we're wondering if we heard them right. After all, truth is stranger than fiction, and the man you love wouldn't expect you to believe such an outrageous and bizarre story if it weren't true, would he?

Well, yes, he would.

Bill was emboldened by Jan's easy acceptance of his previous lies. He knew, based on their experience as a couple, that she would believe almost anything he told her. For her part, Jan continued to be lulled by the sincerity of Bill's explanations for suspicious behavior, even as his stories got more and more illogical.

We were going on a family outing—your basic happy all-American family, right? Bill and I in the front, kids in the back, beautiful day—how could life be any better? I had forgotten my sunglasses, but I always kept an extra pair in the glove compartment of both Bill's and my car. I opened the glove compartment and was taking out the glasses when I noticed a Polaroid picture, face down. I took it out and turned it over. It was a picture of a small, extremely pretty brunette, about thirty, in a tight sweater and blue jeans. She really was a knockout. But what on earth was her picture doing in Bill's car? I showed it to him.

At first he pretended he didn't know who it was. Then he said, "Omigod—it's Carla [his ex-wife]." Then he got really creative. "But how did her picture get into my car? Maybe she's been stalking me. I told you how crazy she is and how obsessed with me. I guess she's been following me and got into the car one of the times I left it in the driveway. I guess this is her way of staying connected with me."

Well, that could happen, couldn't it? That made sense. Unstable ex-wife can't accept that he isn't coming back, so she finds ways to invade his new life and cause trouble between us. I mean, Bill wouldn't lie to me, and he certainly wouldn't still be seeing someone he had so many problems with.

Sometimes it's a sense of invincibility that leads a man to venture into the most outrageous varieties of denial. He's been in control of the information he wants you to have, and, he reasons, he's fully capable of inventing a completely believable reality that will explain away any troubling discoveries you make.

THE CATCH–22 OF DENIAL

Men who deny their lies in the face of strong evidence are trying to convince you that:

- You didn't see what you saw.
- You didn't hear what you heard.
- You don't know what you know.
- You're exaggerating/imagining things/paranoid.
- You're hurting them and ruining your relationship.
- They're not the one with the problem—you are.
- Other people are trying to cause trouble between you.

They offer us a difficult choice. We can convince ourselves through our own denial that we're the ones at fault, that we're over-reacting, or even that we're crazy. If we are successful in this self-delusion, the relationship can go on as it is, and no boats get rocked. Or we can stick to our guns, upset the man we love, and put the relationship in jeopardy. It's self-destructive fantasy vs. a tough, very painful reality. And as we'll see, many of us willingly choose the first path.

THE CONFESSORS

Denying isn't every man's style. Some find it too inconvenient or anxiety-producing to have to invent elaborate stories and try to keep them straight. Others, who are basically decent, with strong consciences, hate the guilt they feel and are extremely uncomfortable with the knowledge that they are hurting their partners and the relationship. Still others just want to get us off their backs and know that confessing is a quick way to do it.

Sometimes the confession is all we hope it will be—a new beginning, a chance to rebuild trust and start again. We'll see couples who use confessions in that way in the second half of this book. But for now, it's important to be aware that confessing can be very seductive. For many men who lie, confessing is often just another tactic for diverting your attention from the magnitude and consequences of their lies. Too often, the man you love confesses, apologizes—and continues to lie.

TECHNIQUE NO. 7: "I WAS A BAD BOY"

- "I can't lie to you—I did it. But it's over and it'll never happen again."
- "I blew it. I'm so sorry. Please forgive me."
- "You have every right to hate me, but please give me another chance."

Compared with the men who lie and then compound things by lying about the lie, the confessor seems like a different breed. He did it, he admits it, and now he claims he wants to make amends. How can we deny him absolution?

Kathy, the vocational nurse, often let herself be thrown off guard by the sweet sound of confessions from her husband, David, who was lying regularly about money:

Soon after we were married, he started buying things with my credit card. Private stuff for his computer and ham radio. At first he would deny it, but when I confronted him with the bills, he broke down and admitted what he'd done. He said he had been embarrassed to ask me for the money directly. Then he told me how he was going to put some money aside each week and pay me back. He said he knew he'd been irresponsible in the past, but he was really turning his life around and it would never happen again. I was very touched, and I felt so proud of him. He wanted to clean up his act. It was music to my ears.

As far as Kathy was concerned, the relationship was back on track. There were no secrets, the misunderstandings had been cleared up, and best of all, David had really opened his heart to her and shared intimate and painful feelings. He loved her; he would change for her. Like so many women, she found it easy to give credence to the words she wanted to hear. Unfortunately, David's actions didn't match his promises.

He would say he was going to work, but I called him one day to ask him something and the receptionist said he hadn't been in all day. When he got home, I told him I knew he didn't go to work. I told him I felt really duped and tricked. He looked very pained and told me he had so much on his mind, he needed to take a mental-health day for himself, so he'd gone to the movies. See—he always confessed, so I thought, "Well, at least he's not lying to me." Besides, he was my best friend. I could tell him anything, and he really listened.

As David found, confessing put him, at least for a time, in the camp of the honorable. He knew that acknowledging the truth went a long way toward ameliorating Kathy's frustration with him. She may have been angry with what he did, but at least, she reasoned, he was man enough to admit it. She totally overlooked the fact that the only reason he was forced to confess was that he had lied to her in the first place.

Wiping the Slate Clean

If a man has a high threshold of guilt, his confessions may come only after he's up to his neck in lies and deception. Men like this often use confession as a license to keep doing exactly what they want.

Allen, Nora's husband, who denied his infidelities with almost the whole repertoire of denial techniques, moved on to another pattern as time went on:

After all the denial and stories, he started confessing. "Yes, it's true—I did have a brief fling with someone at work, but it's over, I swear it, and it'll never happen again. I love you, I love my son—there's no way I want to lose either of you." God, I wanted so much to believe him.

As far as Allen was concerned, confessing was enough to wipe the slate clean. Confessing may be good for the soul of the man who lies—it's just not very good for the woman in his life as long as she allows it to be an end in itself.

Everything would be glorious for about three days. Then I would find another clue. A store receipt for something I knew I never got—things like that. It was almost as if he wanted to get caught. The cycle was always the same. He would cheat on me, I would find out, and then the same pattern. First the denial, then the confession, then the apologies and the promises and the protestations of love and devotion.

Kathy and Nora were both caught up in a confession cycle of their own, going from shock and anger to forgiveness to hope and crushing disappointment when they discovered the next lie.

As they learned, words are just words, and promises of change are meaningless until they're supported by some hard, honest personal growth work that leads to genuine behavioral change. Unfortunately, Kathy and Nora believed that when their partners admitted their misdeeds, they were showing such strength of character that the admissions overshadowed the lies.

TECHNIQUE NO. 8: "IT WAS NO BIG DEAL"

- "What are you getting so upset/hysterical/angry about?"
- "It didn't mean anything."
- "You're overreacting."

With words and demeanor, men who lie to us can convey the impression that a betrayal or an act of deception is relatively unimportant—no need to worry, it's nothing. They encourage us to relax, recognize the lie was harmless, and not make a fuss. They may even give us indications about what they intend to do, making their plans sound so casual that we begin to question our right to be upset. Men who use this technique are masters of minimizing and discounting their actions—no matter how serious they may be—and our reactions to them.

When Lee, the clothing store manager, found out that Barry was living with another woman at the same time he was pursuing her, she was shocked by his response to her discovery.

I was really hurt and angry, but I tried to keep my cool. I told him I didn't appreciate him lying to me, especially since I had been totally honest with him. He acted like it was no big deal—I think he was really convinced that he wasn't doing any-

thing wrong. He justified the whole thing because he claimed he didn't have a future with her—that he wanted something better.

Carol's husband, Ken, was another master minimizer, as he demonstrated when Carol confronted him with her discovery that he'd been jailed after a drug bust:

Part of me was numb, and the other part was homicidal. The minute he walked in from work I screamed at him, "Why didn't you tell me?" I couldn't believe his answer. He said, "It's no big deal. I was young, and it was just pot. I didn't tell you I'd been arrested for it because, even though it happened so long ago, I was afraid you would think I was no good and you wouldn't marry me."

Minimizing is an effective way for a man to avoid taking personal responsibility for the seriousness of his actions and his lies. Ken's lie had cost Carol a job she loved, but to him it was blown all out of proportion. After all, he just did what everyone else was doing and had the bad luck to get arrested. No acknowledgment of the consequences of his behavior, no acknowledgment that he had lied to his wife. Just a casual dismissal of these events with "It's no big deal."

My client Pat, who owns a popular antique shop, was dazed when this technique emerged in her relationship with her boyfriend Paul.

Paul and I had been seeing each other steadily for about five months. It was fun and sexy, and he was really sweet and affectionate—a great guy. I didn't know if the relationship was going anywhere, and that was OK because I was newly divorced and I wasn't about to rush into anything. The one thing we both committed to was that neither of us would see other people as long as we were together. He had his place and I had mine, and that seemed to work for both of us.

One evening he told me that an old girlfriend of his was coming into town for a couple of weeks and had asked if she could stay with him. He assured me that the romance had been over for a long time and that I didn't have to worry about anything sexual happening between them. I told him I wasn't thrilled with the arrangement, but I didn't feel I had a right to tell him not to do it. Besides, good old Pat—I always have to be so understanding and mature. I didn't want to look jealous or possessive.

The messages Paul was giving Pat were decidedly mixed. On the one hand, "An old girlfriend is going to stay with me for two weeks" certainly set off alarm bells for her. On the other hand were Paul's reassurances that the visit wouldn't affect the amount of time he spent with Pat and that everything would be strictly platonic.

So for two weeks we're in our usual pattern of movies, dinners, drives down to the beach, and great sex. Then about a week after she leaves, he calls me, and the minute he said hi, I knew something was wrong. He said he had to talk to me and he couldn't do it over the phone. It was a long twenty minutes before he got there, and I'm thinking, "OK. He wants to get back with her. I'm too independent for him." I was pretty scared and upset. I didn't want to lose him.

He comes over looking pretty serious, and we sit on my patio, and he takes my hand and very quietly tells me he's caught herpes from this woman. "But, but—," I'm sputtering, "you told me there wasn't going to be any sex between you!" And he says, "I know, baby, and I'm really sorry—things just got out of hand." If he'd stopped there it would have been bad enough, but then he gets this crooked little-boy smile on his face and he says the most incredible thing! "Well, honey, you know me. How can I sleep in the same bed with a pretty girl and not have sex with her? Come on! There's no need to get so upset—everything's going to be fine. I've been to the doctor and he told me exactly what to do."

I wanted to strangle him. He never told me they would be sleeping in the same bed! And he's sleeping with me at the same time, and maybe he's infected me too. But what made it so much worse was his acting so casual about it. Is he suggesting I should have stopped him, and so he's not the only one who's responsible? What am I supposed to do now?"

Paul was ready to resume his relationship with Pat as though nothing had happened. Apparently it was no big deal to him that he had conveniently omitted telling Pat that his ex-girlfriend would be sleeping in the same bed with him.

When he couldn't lie about it any longer, he confessed but acted as though what had happened was almost funny. Here's this charming, horny guy who just couldn't help himself. When he said, "You know me," it sounded as though he was suggesting that Pat should have known that something like that was going to happen.

Pat and Paul had agreed to an exclusive relationship, and Paul violated that agreement. Pat may not have felt she had the right to make a big fuss when he told her about his former lover staying with him, but she certainly had the right not to be lied to and to have Paul take his behavior far more seriously than he did. By acting as if lying about sleeping with someone else and getting a sexually transmitted disease were no big deal, he was insulting Pat and their relationship.

Men who tend to minimize and discount bad behavior try to sell us their version of reality by relying on many of the qualities that attracted us to them in the first place—the charm, the smoothness, the confidence. When caught in a lie, they fall back on what worked for them in the past.

Minimizing is crazy-making. It makes us doubt our own perceptions and our right to be angry. We start second-guessing ourselves. Am I overreacting? Am I blowing this out of proportion? Pat was clear-eyed enough not to fall into that trap, but as we'll see in Chapter 5, many women who are dealing with this maddening technique wind up feeling compelled to justify their normal and appropriate reactions to being lied to.

TECHNIQUE NO. 9: "YES, I DID IT, BUT IT'S REALLY YOUR FAULT"

- "You drove me to it."
- "I didn't tell you because you can't handle the truth."
- "I didn't tell you because you get so upset."

If you've always linked confessions with the idea of remorse, this technique will come as a complete surprise. Confessing doesn't always involve having your man open his heart and beg for forgiveness. Some men, when caught in a lie, come out swinging, proving once again that the best defense is a good offense.

Kathy found that David's confessions and promises to reform began to deteriorate over time when David began to lie about behavior he knew was vitally important to her—his drinking:

Two years into the marriage I suspected he was drinking again, but he totally denied it. He started having some pretty severe mood swings and they scared me, so I moved out and went to my sister's. Then one of our cats ran away, and David called me to help him find her. I smelled liquor on his breath and said so. His answer was, "If you hadn't left me, I wouldn't have to drink." Well, I knew that was a total cop-out, but I felt really guilty just the same.

David, like many men caught in a lie, was putting a 180-degree spin on reality to convince his partner that his behavior and lying were really her fault. He was doing classic rationalizing—making excuses to obscure bad behavior: "I only did it because . . ." According to David, he had no choice but to lie to Kathy about his drinking. Why? Because she had made him so miserable. The argument isn't very logical, but it can completely shift our focus and take our attention off the lie and the liar, which is exactly what it's intended to do.

Ken also turned reality on its head when he realized that trying to downplay his arrest wasn't making Carol feel any calmer about losing the job she'd wanted so much. He knew he was in trouble, so he switched from minimizing to blaming:

The first thing he wanted to do was make love. That was always his solution for everything. I told him I was too upset, and he got very petulant. "So you're going to punish me now. See—that's why guys have to lie sometimes—because if they tell the truth, their wives get pissed and won't have sex."

Here are some other familiar examples of the I-only-did-it-because strategy and what they really mean:

- "I didn't think you could handle it if I told you I've been married before/got a child somewhere/used drugs/got the IRS after me." Translation: I only lie because you're so weak.
- "I can't tell you the truth about our finances. You get too hysterical about money problems." Translation: The only reason I lied is that you're so irrational.
- "OK, so I'm having an affair. What do you expect when you're so preoccupied with your career?" Translation: I only did it because you're so self-centered.

Whether a man addresses your questions or suspicions with denial or confession or a combination of the two, his goals are the same: to get you to accept his explanations, back off, end the confrontation, and return to the status quo. He may carefully choose techniques to get you to believe that a serious lie was insignificant or that a pattern of lying was just a one-time mistake. And sometimes he's hardly aware of how manipulative he's being. But when he relies on the techniques we've seen in this chapter, you can be sure of one thing: he's pouring ever-increasing amounts of his life into perpetuating a destructive cycle of lies.

3

The Mind of the Liar

Why does he do it? That's the question that drives most women crazy. Why is it so important to him to keep certain truths from you? If he has a conscience, don't his lies make him feel guilty? And don't they consume more and more of his emotional energy?

Sometimes the answers aren't terribly complicated. He may lie because it seems easier than telling the truth. He may lie because he's greedy and he wants what he wants without having to be accountable to you. He may lie to avoid the unpleasant consequences of telling you the truth about something he knows will incur your disapproval, your frustration, and especially your anger.

But often the causes are complex and more difficult to get to. They may be buried deep in his unconscious world and shaped by all of his prior life experiences, his relationship with his parents and other important people in his life, what he has learned and believes about men and women, and the many fears and conflicts that are outside of his awareness.

I know you're eager to find explanations, but before we start our exploration, it's important to remember two things: First, none of what follows is meant as an excuse or an apology for his lying. He has made a choice to lie even though there are many other options available. That doesn't mean he's a monster or a totally bad guy, but he is responsible for making a choice to deceive and betray you. Telling the truth may be a lot scarier and a lot riskier, but it is the only option that has a chance to take the relationship to a healthier plateau. Second, you can't always find the "why." Cause and effect are often elusive, and as much as you believe you might be comforted by having explanations for his lying, you won't always be able to find them. Certainly, though, some themes come to the forefront, and the more closely we look, the more we can uncover clues about what drives this maddening and destructive behavior.

LIES AS PROTECTION

A man's lies spring from a potent mixture of attitudes, perceptions, and needs intersecting with who he is, where he came from, and what's happening in his life. As we look at what appears to be driving men's lying, we can see that most of their lies are a potent way to ward off feelings and events they consider threatening or painful. A man's lies serve both to protect some of his powerful needs and to shield him from a variety of unpleasant feelings, fears, and consequences. Lying protects:

- The image he wants to project to the world, to you, and to himself
- His need for freedom and autonomy
- His need to be in control

Lying also serves as a protection from some very basic fears:

- His fear that you would leave him if he told you the truth
- His fear that you will dominate him
- His fear of the terrible Cs: conflict, confrontation, and consequences
- His fear of your anger

There's no neat way to separate the threads as we look into what moves a man to lie. The needs and fears are interwoven. And keep in mind that some lies are situational and opportunistic: he sees a chance to win, gain an advantage, or spare himself some discomfort or effort, so he grabs it. But when lying becomes a deeply ingrained part of his behavior, it's usually because these needs and fears have come together in a way that makes lying seem not only convenient for him but almost mandatory.

PROTECTING HIS IMAGE

Many men who lie are playing to three audiences—you, the world at large, and themselves. In order to project a positive image of himself as Mr. Wonderful—honorable, caring, decent, successful—and to have the freedom to keep doing what he wants to do, he often has to do some masterly truth-juggling.

When Jan, the graphic designer, let Bill know about the disturbing phone call from Carla and asked him if it was true that he'd actually been married twice before, Bill denied everything. And later, when she found a picture of Carla in the glove compartment, he invented a wild story to cover himself.

I found out the truth about six months later when we were buying a house and were filling out the escrow papers. Bill gave me the documents and told me to fill out my part and he'd take care of his. I was going through a drawer in his desk to get some stamps and I saw the application. There's a place where you list all previous marriages, and sure enough, there was his first marriage and his second to "Carla Morton." I can't even describe how I felt—sick, mainly, and totally off balance. He won't lie to an escrow company, because that's illegal, but it's OK to lie to me? I insisted that he just tell me the truth—the whole truth—this time.

The discovery was inevitable. When his lies were found out and denial wasn't going to work anymore, Bill launched into some skillful image control:

He put his arms around me and said he was so sorry he hadn't told me the truth about Carla. Yes, they'd been married, but it was only for a few months. He never planned to marry her and only did because she was pregnant and she begged him

*to do the right thing and give their baby a name. He said that
Carla had a miscarriage and went a little nuts and had to be
hospitalized for depression, and he waited until she was better
and stabilized on medication before he divorced her. He said he
hadn't told me because he was afraid he'd lose me. He was
afraid if I knew he'd been married twice I might think he was a
bad risk and change my mind.*

*Everything he said seemed perfectly logical and reasonable.
He had tears in his eyes. By the time he got through, I thought he
was the most honorable, caring man in the world. How many
men in this day and age would marry someone just because
she'd gotten pregnant, and then stand by her through all her problems? In my mind he was practically a candidate for sainthood.*

Well, not quite. Bill took pains to explain his lie in almost
heroic terms, and in so doing he successfully put considerable
distance between himself and his lies. But Bill's belief that he
would somehow look better to Jan by lying to her, and then compounding the first lie with another, defies logic.

One clue to his thinking is in Bill's statement that he was
afraid he would lose Jan if she knew the truth. Many men will lie
to make themselves look better in order to avoid rejection. They
polish their images by hiding many things about who they are
and what they've done in order to get you to bond with them, figuring they'll deal with the lies if and when they get discovered.

Jan provided some additional clues:

*Bill's always gotten by on his looks and charm. He'd been a
Big Man on Campus, elected to every office he ever ran for in
college, and people admired and adored him—especially
women. He was used to getting what he wanted without having
to work very hard for it. But I noticed he was always overly
concerned with what people thought about him.*

Bill's carefully constructed image fed his ego and was his
ticket to success. Anything that threatened that image—like two
failed marriages—would have to remain invisible or, if necessary,
be explained in a way that would continue to protect that image.

Bill probably believed he wouldn't be accepted if he had any flaws. Running through his head were warnings that sounded something like this:

- If she really knew the truth about me, she'd dump me.
- She won't love me if I'm not perfect.
- She'll never forgive me for my mistakes or weaknesses, so I have to hide them.

THE TRUTH IS NOT MY FRIEND

Jan stopped romanticizing Bill's lies and saw them for what they were, and that shift precipitated a crisis in their marriage—a crisis that motivated them to go into couples counseling.

During one of our sessions, I asked Bill if he had any idea where he got the notion that if he told the truth, the consequences would be worse than lying.

It's funny I didn't think of this before. My father was always doing a real bait-and-switch number on me when I was a kid. He had this way of setting me up by telling me that nothing bad would happen if I told him the truth, and when I was sucker enough to believe him he'd turn around and punish me. One time really stands out in my mind, but he would do this a lot. It was Christmas morning . . . I was about ten. I'd nicked the side of his car with my brand-new bike, and I prayed he wouldn't notice it, but of course he did. He asked me what I knew about the door ding and I just stood there with my hands in my pockets, not saying anything. He said, "Just tell me the truth about what happened. It's not a problem for me if you just tell me the truth." Finally, I admitted I'd done it when I took my bike out of the garage. He was quiet for a minute and then he said, "Well, that bike will just about pay for the repairs, so it's going back to the store, and maybe that will teach you to be careful of other people's things." Well, I finally got smart and swore to myself nobody was ever going to trick me and make me look bad like that again.

When Jan had said to Bill, "Just tell me the truth," she had no way of knowing that she was activating powerful memories for him—memories that had formed the basis of equally powerful beliefs about what happens when you tell the truth. When Bill's father lied to him and set him up to be humiliated and punished for being truthful, his son came to conclusions that stayed with him into his adult life:

- The truth gets powerful people angry with you.
- The truth gets you punished.
- The truth makes you look bad.
- Don't trust people when they say, "Just tell me the truth."
- You've got nothing to gain and everything to lose by admitting mistakes.
- The people (like father) who lie have the power.

When Bill's belief that lying was the safer—and smarter—option mixed with his need to always look good and be seen as a great guy, the truth didn't stand much of a chance. And if both Bill and Jan were not willing to do something about it, neither did their marriage.

THE LIE OF "EVERYTHING'S FINE"

The quest for a great image leads some men down the path of lying about money and living beyond their means in order to impress everyone, including you, with how successful and smart they are. When the image your lover is cultivating to get people to admire him doesn't mesh with reality, you'll find that your life becomes a house of cards.

Diane, the paralegal whose husband, Ben, had lied to her about giving money to his daughter, also became intimately familiar with the lies that become part of everyday life with a man who is trying to create the image that he's made it big. Ben was in a business that put him around a lot of wealthy people:

There's so much posturing in business that I just accepted it as going with the territory. I've heard Ben at parties talking about deals as if they were all nailed down when they were far from it. Just recently he was telling people about how he was going to develop condos in Malibu and it would make him millions. I knew he'd been paying an architect to draw up plans, but he didn't even have title to the land yet. It was all smoke and mirrors.

Ben was puffing himself up to anyone who would listen to him about his various real estate ventures. In that way he could look like a successful entrepreneur—which he was certain would get him the acceptance and admiration he so fervently wanted. And to top it all off, Diane learned that he was also lying to her about where almost all of their money was going. As so often happens, she had to find out from someone else:

Ben's secretary was leaving after working for him for almost ten years. About a week before she went, she called me. She said, "I know I'm probably out of line here, but I just had to tell you that you really need to get Ben to tell you about what's happening with your money." I felt really scared because we have a lot of debts—we live way beyond our means. He always has to have a new car and hand-tailored suits, and he's always the first one to reach for the check—you know the type. But he's always assuring me everything's fine and there's no problem. I asked her what she meant and she said that Ben had been buying land all over the place for spec deals and borrowing money at very high interest rates to pay for it all. Now he's getting loans to repay the loans and to cover the overhead for the business. She said she hadn't been paid for over a month, and that's why she has to leave. And all he says is, "Everything's fine." My god, Susan. I'm totally panicked.

Everything wasn't fine. Ben's world was spinning out of control, and Diane was suddenly confronted with how Ben's grandiosity had pushed them right to the edge of the cliff. Ben consistently refused to admit any problems to her because that would make him look weak. Well dressed and smooth talking, Ben knew how to make an impression. But he hadn't figured out that the driving force behind his lies was a conviction that he wasn't OK just being himself. He had to create an image that was impossible for him to live up to. Like a little boy putting on his father's shoes and pretending to be grown-up, Ben was playing a role and telling whatever lies would enhance that role, to himself, to Diane, and to friends and associates.

A COMPARTMENT FOR EVERYTHING

A very different kind of image management occurs with a man who may be doing just fine professionally but leading a less than honest personal life. Men like this become experts in compartmentalizing. Career is in one compartment, wife and family in a second compartment, and the other woman (or women) in yet another.

Gwen, a medical researcher, has had a two-year relationship with the medical director of the hospital where she works. Peter is highly regarded in his profession for his compassion, skill, and ethics.

The thing that puzzles me is that he's totally honorable in every part of his life—except for his relationship with his wife. He's been married since he was twenty to a woman who's a few years older than he is and looks like his mother. When we first started seeing each other, he was totally honest about the boundaries. He said he would never leave his wife or kids. He said he doesn't love his wife, but he won't leave her either. So he has affairs. Some of them have lasted for several years. I'm not his first affair, and I know I won't be his last, but I'm really crazy about him. I asked him, "How can you live like this?" and he said, "I have an obligation to these people to take care of them. If I left, it would tear them apart and it would destroy my parents—and I'm not in the business of hurting people I care about. So I'm not leaving. I work hard and I'm proud of what I've accomplished, but I do feel entitled to some pleasure and happiness." I know I have to end it because this is a dead-end street for me, but I just can't understand how he can live like that.

Peter can live like that because he is a master compartmentalizer. He can avoid being overcome with guilt about his lies and affairs by separating them from the rest of his life. In this way he is able to maintain his image as a dutiful and conscientious son, husband, and father, and through his work, he makes an important contribution to society. He is convinced that as long as no one knows about the other part of his life, no one is hurt and it has no effect on his family's well-being.

THE GOLDEN BOY

I learned from Gwen that Peter has always had people depending on him, and he clings tightly to the image of himself as the bulwark of his family:

He's always been the one who held things together—a sort of golden boy. His parents are very simple, uneducated people from the Midwest, and here he's this kid who helped out by working after school and turns out to be this genius who really became a superstar in his field. They're always telling him how proud they are of him and how much joy they get from his marriage and their grandchildren. He even bought a house for them here so they could be closer to him. But he never got to play or be a kid. It's been work, work, work and duty, duty, duty.

My guess is that Peter feels trapped by a sense of obligation drilled into him from the time he was young, and as long as he's honoring it, he can justify lying to his wife as the kinder and more benign option. If he were to own up to his unhappiness in his marriage, he'd upend his family and undoubtedly cause incalculable distress. He would also blow his image as Mr. Responsible. So instead he has affairs, which provide enough excitement and satisfaction to dilute his need to do anything about his situation at home. Yes, Peter is very responsible and honorable in many parts of his life, but by choosing to lead a double life, he's never fully committed to anyone—least of all himself.

It takes a lot of courage to show your true self to another person, but men who need to maintain a certain image choose another route. And in so doing, they almost ensure that they will not be loved for their true selves and that the intimacy you both want will inevitably be a casualty of their charade.

HIS NEED FOR FREEDOM AND AUTONOMY: THE INTERNAL WAR OF INDEPENDENCE

At the core of many men's lies to women is a primal push-pull that makes their feelings toward us both confusing and ambivalent. They want to be connected and loved, but they also want their autonomy. For many men, these wants are constantly at war with each other, and their need to persuade themselves that they're not emotionally dependent becomes a lifelong struggle that's painful for them and frustrating for us.

The battle begins in childhood, when a little boy must push away from his mother and identify with his father in order to define his maleness. Being male means standing on his own two feet, cutting the apron strings, and not being a "mama's boy." But because his mother is his first source of nurturing and comfort, he hungers to reconnect with her. That hunger is balanced by strong fears and shame. Being a man means being separate from Mom—and by extension all other women.

As boys develop, they enter an extremely chaotic period of life—adolescence, a time of intense secrecy and turmoil. Struggling to establish their own boundaries and sense of self, many boys may lie about everything: where they've been, who they've been with, where they're going, what they're thinking and feeling.

Getting out from under the thumb of parental control is part of a rite of passage that often involves drinking too much, staying up all night, or building macho credentials by racking up as many sexual conquests as possible. Sounds a lot like some of the men we've already met in this book, doesn't it?

Eventually, some young men fumble their way past mere braggadocio and toward behaviors that will allow them to have reasonably healthy relationships with women. But other men never seem to figure out how to get the love and comfort they want from women while ensuring that they don't feel dominated or engulfed. For them, the battles of adolescence seem to continue through their adult lives, with their partner cast in the role of the symbolic parent.

David, the carpenter who was married to Kathy, the nurse we met in Chapter 1, grew up in a world of women who treated him like a prince:

His father died when he was little, and though he was the youngest child in the family, he was the only boy. From what his sisters have told me, their mom was almost deferential to him. They all had little jobs to earn spending money, but he was a kind of sickly kid and couldn't mow lawns because he had allergies. Couldn't take time away from his homework to work flipping burgers. Everything he got was given to him, and he had this pack of women always protecting him. He was kind of spoiled, and definitely sheltered from almost every kind of responsibility. They could never see that anything he did was his fault, and if he made a mess in his life, someone would just come along and clean up after him.

Fast-forward to adulthood.

Women had always been David's safety net. When he married Kathy, he had strong expectations that he might not even have been aware of, that this was the way it was supposed to be.

I kept finding new bills from his spending sprees. I was the major wage earner, and I guess somehow he expected things would magically get paid off. When I confronted him, he would say things like "I don't have to ask your permission every time I want to spend some money. I'll take care of it." See, I think the things he bought gave him some kind of status. He was always afraid people wouldn't like him. He felt very inadequate and inferior.

Kathy was very insightful in her evaluation of how David's spending sprees temporarily served to reassure him that he was making his own decisions and that he wasn't the wimp he feared being. Kathy, as a strong, competent woman, created a lot of inner turmoil for David. Their life together was full of reminders of how he'd always depended on the women in his life to take care of him. David needed Kathy both emotionally and financially, but he was ashamed of those needs, so he found ways to establish his masculinity by asserting himself through buying things and then lying about it. When he was found out, he would first become defiant—his way of fighting against the deep dependency on women that had always made him feel less than a man.

ANGER VS. SPITE

Phil and Helen, a handsome couple in their late forties with grown children, wanted help to salvage a marriage that was coming apart at the seams because of what Helen called Phil's "secret life":

It's the damn computer. He said he wanted it for paperwork he was bringing home—that was the first lie. I didn't know what was going on at first, but he was spending an awful lot of time "working." One night I brought him a cup of coffee and I couldn't believe what I saw on that screen. He clicked a few buttons really fast and tried to make it disappear, but I got a good look, and it was disgusting. He'd been typing really graphic sex stuff, and someone was typing messages back. It turned out he'd been spending hours in these chat rooms, probably jerking off. He was very embarrassed, and he said if it was upsetting me so much he'd stop.

But Phil didn't stop. One night Helen woke around two in the morning and realized Phil wasn't in bed. She found him at the computer.

Phil admitted he'd become heavily involved in the world of on-line sex.

Sure I get off on it. But it's not like I'm some low-life going to dirty movies. She makes me sound like a pervert, but I'm a responsible guy. I can't spend every minute of my life doing what she wants me to do.

By the time Helen and Phil came to see me, they'd been caught in a tug-of-war over cybersex for months. And the more Helen nagged Phil to stop, the more he wanted to be in that chat room. He'd promise to quit to appease her, but inevitably she'd find that his promises had been broken.

He's just so weak I can't stand it. He's got no self-control. It's as bad as if he was having an affair.

Helen, frustrated and angry over being lied to, had turned to berating Phil, which only pushed him more firmly into the very behavior she was trying to stop. By labeling Phil as weak and showing her contempt for him, she had moved into the role of critical mother. This only increased Phil's need to rebel against her to prove his autonomy.

DON'T GET CAUGHT

There were interesting parallels between Phil's relationship to his mother in adolescence and the scenario that he played out with his wife:

I grew up in a strict Baptist household—we were at church practically every day. I guess you could say my mother was the enforcer. No dancing, no dating till we were sixteen. You can imagine what happened when she found a copy of Penthouse under my mattress when I was fourteen. She was livid. I was dragged in to talk to the pastor and it was pretty humiliating— I probably still know the passages from the Bible about various "abominations" that he made me memorize. So I learned that the best thing to do was smile, play along, and don't get caught. If anything, those magazines became more important to me. I probably snuck around even more after that.

Phil was mortified by the experience with his mother and the minister and pretended to shove his burgeoning interest in sex under the rug. I'm not saying this was the sole genesis of his secretive behavior as an adult, but it certainly played a part. When Helen, who tended to be overbearing and belittling, criticized him about something sex-related, she inadvertently assumed the role of the mother of his adolescent memory—the woman you have to hide everything from and defy.

As Phil put it:

I just think, Screw you! What's the big deal here? Is this all she cares about? It's not hurting her. I'm entitled to some relaxation.

But the power struggle over Phil's "relaxation" was hurting the marriage. The couple had become remote, scarcely speaking, much less touching or making love. Phil's interest in on-line sex might have been harmless at the beginning, but it had escalated to the point where fantasy had replaced reality and become a substitute for a real relationship. Now the conflict wasn't just about chat rooms. It was about Phil's need to prove that his wife didn't control him.

They were locked in a cycle in which Phil lied to Helen, Helen found out and got angry and critical, Phil withdrew, rebelled, and lied more.

THE FEAR OF WOMEN'S ANGER

I pointed out to Phil that a lot of other choices were available to him. He could, for example, negotiate a compromise with Helen regarding the amount of time he spent in the chat room. Or if he wanted to go to the wall with it, he could defy her directly instead of sneaking around and lying about what he was doing. I wasn't recommending that as the best solution, but his reaction to this option was significant.

Phil: There's no way I can do that.
Susan: How come?
Phil: You've never seen her when she gets angry.
Susan: That's true—tell me what happens.
Phil: It's awful—her face gets red and her eyes narrow and . . .
   I don't know . . . I just can't deal with it.
Susan: When Helen gets angry it makes me feel. . . . Finish the sentence.

Phil: When Helen gets angry it makes me feel . . . helpless—
that's the best word I can think of.

For many men, even those who appear to be models of power
and success—Phil is a bank vice-president—women's anger
launches them into the unknown. How far will she go? Will she
lose control? If she's angry, does that mean she doesn't love me
anymore? And the most frightening thought of all: if she's angry,
does that mean she will leave me?

Phil wanted his cybersex, but he wanted his marriage too—
and in his mind, Helen's anger meant that the marriage was in
jeopardy. He believed that lying was greatly preferable to any
kind of direct confrontation with her.

Kathy reported a similar reaction from David to a rare out-
burst of frustration on her part. As Kathy tells it:

*After all the promises, I found out he'd forged my signature
to get a credit card, and I just lost it. I screamed at him, called
him a bum, and threatened to leave him. He just collapsed, like
a whipped puppy. He'd been kind of belligerent, but he just
crumbled. He begged me to calm down. He seemed really
shaken—and scared.*

I told Kathy that I had spent a lot of my life being afraid of
men's anger and doing just about anything to avoid it. It never
occurred to me until I became a therapist and had the opportunity to get into the inner world of a lot of men that the opposite
might be true as well. It came as a great revelation to me when I
discovered how deep this fear was and how often men would
choose to lie rather than deal with an angry woman.

SOURCES OF THE FEAR

Certainly some women are very scary when they're angry. But
many women have a difficult time expressing any anger or bend
over backward to be the calm and understanding peacemaker.
Men's fears of women's anger seem to be incomprehensible.

Some of the answers lie, as we've already seen, in a man's relationship with the first woman in his life, his mother, and in his sub-

sequent experiences with all the women who have played an important role in the formation of his feelings and beliefs. Abandonment fears, the pain of rejection or abuse, overprotectiveness, or neglect shape many of his attitudes toward women. But not all. Let's look at another possible source—one that we may tend to overlook if we focus only on his early years.

Woven through mythology, folklore, literature, and art for thousands of years is the archetype of woman as both nurturer and avenging fury who will destroy you if you cross her. Almost every man carries these powerful images with him, usually beneath his conscious awareness. When events in his life activate these images, he is suddenly not responding to the woman in front of him but the larger-than-life Fury whose earthquake and lightning-lit side he definitely doesn't want to set off.

Phil and David were not unique. Many men have told me that an encounter with an angry woman makes them feel helpless, little, and frightened. But we know these feelings are unacceptable to most men, so they push them down and find behaviors that help them prove to themselves that they are not afraid. They may be defiant, or they may be deferential, but it's surprising how many men believe that the best way to avoid your anger is to retreat from the truth that they know will, or already has, angered you, into the protective land of lies.

The great paradox here is that in an attempt to avoid your anger by lying, he will ultimately incur twice as much anger once his lies are discovered. His actions may have been bad enough, but it's the lying about them that really creates the rage he so fears.

THE NEED FOR CONTROL

Sometimes a preemptive strike seems like the best way to manage both his fear of your anger and that difficult struggle between his need for you and his ambivalence about that need. Some men will fend off their partner's anger with intimidating anger of their own and assume control over many aspects of their partner's life. As they see it, the only way to have power and independence is to take them away from you. Lies become a means of proving to themselves that they're top dog; they'll decide who calls the shots, what you can know and not know.

As Ben's world became more and more chaotic, he bore down harder at home. As Diane told me:

I put my own money into our joint account so I could be sure there was always enough to cover the mortgage and other "must pays." Ben insisted on being the one to pay most of the bills, and it didn't seem important enough to argue about. The other day I found a whole stack of unpaid bills in his sock drawer when I was putting the laundry away, including two overdue house payments that he swore he'd made. When I asked him about it he went into a tirade—how I didn't understand anything about business, that I should keep my nose out of things, he would decide what gets paid and when, and I should stick to what I knew how to do. It gets worse. You know that land deal I told you about? Well, I found out he used our savings to pay the architect for plans but couldn't tie down the land. So now we own twenty thousand dollars' worth of plans to nothing.

Ben was trying to support an expensive lifestyle, but his income couldn't keep pace with his bad business decisions. He couldn't admit to any needs or weaknesses. Instead he appointed himself the gatekeeper of all financial information in the relationship, even though Diane was the one who kept bailing them out.

Instead of telling Diane the truth about what was going on so that they could do some problem-solving together, he kept up a confident front, and at the same time he belittled his wife. By playing the control card and withholding vitally important information from her, he could manage, for a little while, to feel in charge.

THE DARKEST SIDE OF CONTROL

Carol, the legal secretary who had lost a wonderful job because of her husband's lies about his unsavory past, became the target of his extreme attempts to show who was the boss early in their marriage:

During our first year together, he wasn't drinking at all. He swore to me that he was through with drinking. But one night one of his old drug buddies came by, and he celebrated by getting drunk and staying out until three in the morning. When I told him I couldn't bear his lying to me and that I'd been frantic with worry and he should have called me, he looked me straight in the eye and said, "I don't have to account to you for anything."

For Ken, being in control meant not only deceiving his wife but insulting and demeaning her as well. He could then beat his chest like King Kong and convince himself that he was a big man.

Soon, Ken's verbal abuse slid over the line.

He was really like two different people. He started to get scary when I confronted him about any of his lies—about drinking, about the drug stuff. He would scream insults at me, calling me a stupid bitch, and if I was lucky he would storm off. If I wasn't lucky, he'd start slamming doors and throwing things and pushing me around. I swore I would leave him, and every time I made an effort in that direction he would panic. He'd tell me how sorry he was and how glad he was we had the baby. He'd promise to respect me. Sometimes he'd cry and say he couldn't live without me. He even got the Bible and swore an oath he would quit drinking, quit hanging around with the guys who got him in trouble, and he'd never raise a hand to me again. And I'd believe him.

I'd quit my job when the baby was born, and I was totally financially dependent on him. He was a good provider. He always worked steadily and took care of us. So we'd make up, make love, and everything would be OK for a while. You know, in those days no one talked about these things, and I thought if I didn't get punched or beaten I wasn't being abused. I just thought I was supposed to be a good wife and figure out how to make him happy so he'd be nicer to me.

Ken's need to control Carol to ensure that she would be too helpless and defeated to leave him was clear in his pattern of psychological and physical abuse. He couldn't bear the thought of losing Carol, but he also couldn't stand to admit to himself how dependent he was on her. When he added intimidation to the lying, it gave him an illusion of power and control. But when he became frightened that he'd gone too far, he placated her with apologies and promises. As with almost all abusive and controlling men, the apologies were hollow, and his promises and protestations of love were all lies.

THE TANGLED WEB

I live in Los Angeles, where the ground looks solid but the deep layers of the earth are crisscrossed with cracks, much like the shell of a hard-boiled egg you've pressed between your palms. When pressure builds on the fault lines, the earth shakes. Deep in the psyche of the man who lies there is a similar condition. He may look solid on the outside, but there are networks of invisible weaknesses and fears. When something activates them, he feels an internal earthquake and opts to lie rather than risk the uproar he's sure telling the truth will create.

For a man who tells and lives lies, lying allows the status quo to continue, at least for a while, because he's convinced that lying prevents you from making a discovery that might cause you to end the relationship. No matter what he's doing or how badly it affects you, don't ever forget: *your leaving is the last thing he wants*.

Sometimes this deep need to stay connected to you can be the catalyst for rebuilding a relationship that has been scarred with lies. And it's what sets many men who lie apart from the dangerous and destructive men you are about to meet—men who are incapable of true connection and whose goal is to cheat and exploit you.

4

The Sociopath

A frog was preparing to swim from one bank of a river to the other. Just as he was about to enter the water, a scorpion came by and begged to ride on his back since, of course, the scorpion couldn't swim.

"Oh, no!" said the frog. "If I let you ride on my back, I know just what will happen. As soon as we get to the other side and you don't need me any more, you'll sting me and I'll die."

"I give you my solemn promise I won't do that," the scorpion assured him. "I really need to get to the other side of the river, and I will be very grateful to you."

Apprehensive, but taking the scorpion at his word, the frog let the scorpion climb onto his back and swam across the river. The moment they reached dry land, the scorpion sank his tail into the frog and released his venom. As the frog was gasping his last breath, he looked forlornly at the scorpion and asked feebly, "Why did you do that?"

"Because," answered the scorpion calmly, "that's what I do."

This chapter is about scorpions in human form, and continuous, remorseless lying is "what they do." They lie to the women they're with, and to just about everyone else. They cheat repeatedly on the women they're married to, they steal from the woman they profess their love for. Their greatest thrill, their highest high, is pulling the wool over the eyes of the women who love and trust them, and they do it without a moment of concern for their targets. This chapter is about the one kind of liar you must leave immediately. It is about sociopaths.

I know you've heard this term before, and it probably brings to mind criminals, wife beaters, even murderers. Certainly there are many sociopaths in those categories, but there are also sociopaths who masquerade as perfectly normal men—men who travel in our social circles and with whom we often fall in love. Unfortunately, very few women really understand who the sociopath is, what he wants, and how he goes about getting it.

The sociopath is different from other men who lie to you. Sociopaths lie chronically and repetitively about the past, the present, and the future. Because lying is an addiction for them, their most intense high, they lie even when the truth is a better story. They continue to lie even after they're caught, and the only remorse they are capable of feeling is for having been found out. They lie for the love of the con, for putting one over on you, and to remind themselves that they're smarter than all those suckers out there who fall for their lies. "Catch me if you can" is what they all seem to be saying.

IT CAN HAPPEN TO YOU

At this point you may be wondering why I'm devoting a separate chapter to this kind of liar. You may believe that you're too smart or too savvy to be taken in by a smooth line or a false facade. You know you're careful, and not gullible, so why would they target you? Besides, isn't it pretty easy to spot people as extreme as sociopaths and to keep them out of your life? And aren't we talking about a tiny percentage of men, anyway?

I wish I could answer those last two questions with a resounding yes, but I can't. I wish predators like the men in this chapter came from identifiable groups or places, and that I could protect you from them by telling you what to avoid. But contrary to what you may believe, they are often not the dregs of society. In fact, they are frequently doctors, lawyers, teachers, clerics, and corporate executives as well as plumbers, salesmen, and bus drivers.

I wish they were a rare breed too. But I can tell you without fear of contradiction, as someone who has spent over twenty years as a trusted advocate for women, that millions of women will, at some time in their lives, become involved with a sociopath. That involvement may be brief or lengthy, but an awful lot of women—even bright, hip, successful, psychologically aware women—get trapped in the invisible web of deception spun by such men. Don't forget for a moment that all sociopaths have one vital thing in common: an extraordinary ability to win the loyalty and devotion of the woman they exploit.

THE SOCIOPATH CHECKLIST

Let me lay out for you the behavioral characteristics that define these men so that there's no confusion regarding what I'm talking about. Astoundingly, just about every sociopath will exhibit most, if not all, of these traits:

- Glib and persuasive
- Highly impulsive, restless, and easily bored, needing constant stimulation
- Practiced at using protestations of love and devotion to get what he wants
- Without feelings of guilt or anxiety
- Full of fake repentance and promises to do better when caught lying
- Often presenting credible business schemes that will return a large payoff if he can just get X dollars from you to get them going
- Totally lacking in conscience
- Vague and inconsistent about his past
- Unable to learn from experience
- Always blaming others for his failures
- Unable to bond closely, cheating repeatedly on his partners
- Insistent on unconditional support and understanding, meeting any questioning with accusations that you are untrusting and unloving

If you look at the first six items on this list, you can see how a man like this might be attractive—even highly attractive—until his dark aspects begin to bleed through the surface. He's a persuasive guy who's never at a loss for words, a man who loves excitement—maybe he's a rock climber or extreme skier or a car racer or a risk-taking businessman. He speaks words of love that sound fabulous, and he seems completely devoted to making you happy. He's calm, not shifty, and confident—never anxious or guilty. If he makes a blunder, he sounds sincerely sorry, and his promises are just what you want to hear.

It's the breaks in the facade that begin to feel frightening. That love of excitement that makes him so much fun, so much more alive than the dull run-of-the-mill men you've encountered, reveals itself to be an impulsive streak that leads him to act without thinking. His great business ideas somehow don't come together, and he's full of blame for others—then repeats the same mistakes again. He's cruel without remorse. Suddenly he's cold as ice. You discover his affairs and the blank spots in his history that he's never filled in. You discover the scams. And if you complain, he blames you for not being there for him.

If you have even a glimmer of suspicion that you are with a man like this, or are still reeling from a recent relationship with one, this chapter may be difficult for you to read. It will probably stir up strong feelings of hurt, anger, and self-reproach. But I urge you to dig deep within yourself for the courage to face the truth about what has been happening to you, or what may have happened in a previous relationship. Understanding sociopaths can be an insurance policy against hooking up with a man like this any time in the future. The truth is always your ally, no matter how tough it may be to face it. This chapter is your wake-up call.

THE MAN WITHOUT A HEART

There are diseases of the body. There are diseases of the mind. The sociopath has a disease of the conscience. The sociopath has big missing pieces inside of him, yet as we have said, he may be the best and most romantic lover you've ever had. But despite his charm and the aura of excitement and drama that often surrounds him, he is incapable of love. He acts with no concern for anyone or anything but his own gratification. He lies for the kick of it. You are not a person but an object to him. A means to an end.

Does this sound scary? I hope so. Because if you are involved with a sociopath, he may be courting you, but you are certainly courting disaster. My friend Diana, a smart, pretty, and generous woman, fell in love with a man like this, and it almost devastated her comfortable, stable life.

The Wizard of Woo

Diana is a publicist for a large California public-relations firm. Divorced, with four teenage children, she was in her early fifties when some mutual friends introduced her to Hank:

"We'd been out a few times and had a terrific time together. It was fun to have fun again, and I didn't ask a whole lot of questions. I wasn't real sure what he did for a living, but I knew it had something to do with investments. He had a new car and always seemed to have plenty of money to spend.

About a month after we'd started seeing each other, I had to go in for foot surgery. The day I came home, he called to see how I was doing. I told him I was tired and feeling a little down. He asked if he could come over and cheer me up. I was thrilled. Here was someone who really cared. My heart was pounding when he came into my room. The next thing I knew he was on the edge of my bed holding my hand and telling me how he wanted to take care of me forever—how I shouldn't be in this big house with just my kids. Something inside me was telling me that things were moving too fast, but I didn't want to listen to that voice right then. I was terribly attracted to him, and I wasn't about to let anything spoil that.

Seduction and deception are the twin hallmarks of the sociopath. Once the beguiling begins, it's a time of intense, overwhelming romantic and sexual excitement—the same kind of intensity and excitement that can mark the beginning of a great relationship. All of us are wary when there's a sense of too much too soon because it may be an indication that something's not quite right, but aside from her slight uneasiness with how quickly things were moving, there was no way for Diana to know for sure that Hank's agenda included something a lot more sinister than romance.

Hidden Agendas

Men like Hank are masters at wooing the women they have zeroed in on, and they're so intense that the targets of their drama will willingly suspend any concerns or feelings of uneasiness.

In many cases a sociopath will detect a window of vulnerability—a small rip in the woman's emotional fabric. Diana, for example, had recently been through an unpleasant divorce and was raising four children on her own. She wanted very much to love someone again and have him love her. Adding to her vulnerability, she had just had surgery that knocked her off her feet, literally and figuratively. Hank registered everything, and it wasn't long before he made his move.

He started staying over a lot, and he said it was silly for us to keep two places, so I told him to move in. He began to ask me about my investments and how much they were paying. I was with a fairly conservative investment firm but I felt safe with them. Hank told me that he'd helped many clients double their money in less than a year, and he could certainly do the same for the woman he loved. I saw him get up early to start watching the market, and sometimes he would be at his computer for hours. He was constantly telling me how much he was making for his clients, so I felt comfortable turning my portfolio over to him. I was in love and I was going to be rich to boot.

But after six months of questioning Hank about her investments and getting vague, evasive reassurances that "everything is looking great," Diana woke up to find his closet empty and no sign of him anywhere. In panic, she called the brokerage house where her account was supposed to be, only to be told they had no record of any account in her name. Hank was gone and so was her entire savings of $175,000.

Classic sociopaths like Hank always leave a trail of misery, heartache, fraud, and debt in their wake. They take what they want when they want it, and they often move on without warning when the woman they're with starts to get suspicious, or when they've gotten all they can from her.

The police were able to locate Hank, who was already living with another woman, and after some time Diana was able to recoup a portion of her money. It was repaid to her by Hank's new victim, a wealthy widow. But it took longer for her to recoup her confidence and self-respect. Her broken heart, and her self-doubt and suspicion, are still healing.

THE BEST ACTORS IN THE WORLD

Hank looked great on the surface because he was, like all sociopaths, just what his victim wanted him to be. Sociopaths are extremely persuasive because every bit of their energy goes into creating the aura of intimacy. Most of us, in courting, have a whole range of questions and concerns, everything from "Are we compatible?" to "Does my hair look all right?" But the sociopath is single-mindedly concerned with the question "How am I coming across?" With no worries about making a genuine connection, he fine-tunes his presentation, custom designing it for you. And if he needs to, he can play a completely different role with his next target.

My client Laurie gave me a classic example of how smoothly a man like this can slip into roles and costumes. A thirty-eight-year-old sculptor and teacher, Laurie came to see me after a year-and-a-half relationship with a thirty-nine-year-old marriage and family counselor named Michael:

He was still legally married when we started seeing each other, but he assured me he was ready to file for divorce. He told me the only thing that had held him back was his seven-year-old son. I thought he was this wonderful man who had some problems to work through and then we could be together. He gave me so much. All I wanted was someone who was kind to me, and Michael zeroed in on that. He would put on this facade of caring. He would go into his therapist mode with me. He'd put on a cardigan sweater and baggy corduroy pants and urge me to talk to him about my feelings and my problems. When I

*would tell him about some of the painful things that happened
to me as a child, he would say things like "That must have been
terrible for you" or "You must have really been hurt by that." I
felt so connected to him, and so validated.*

Sounds wonderful, doesn't it? A sensitive, understanding man
who really listens and feels your pain. Michael even dressed the
part. So what's wrong with this picture? What's wrong is that this
was just a role Michael played to keep Laurie hooked into a
chaotic and destructive relationship. It had nothing at all to do
with who Michael really was. With the sociopath, what you see is
definitely not what you get.

THRIVING ON CHAOS

What Laurie got was eighteen months of madness during which
time she discovered things about Michael that made her wonder
sometimes if she was going crazy:

*As a result of what I saw as the very positive side of our
relationship, I developed a high level of tolerance for his lying.
He would tell me how much he loved me and what a great life
we were going to have together and what a witch his wife was.
Then out of the blue he says, "I don't see a future with you—
you're not marriage material." And he moves out and goes back
to his wife! Two months later, he calls and says he can't live
without me and he made a mistake and it's all over with Karen
and him and can he come back. So of course I say yes. That
went on for the whole time we were together. Every time I
thought we were really getting it together, he would find some
reason why it wasn't working between us and go back to Karen.
Two months seemed to be his pattern. Two months with her, two
months with me. I felt like a yo-yo—come here, go away, I want
you, I don't want you. But I loved the "I want you."*

Whenever things got too quiet for Michael he would create an
uproar. He bounced back and forth between his wife and his girlfriend, lying to each of them and creating havoc in both their lives,
without ever considering how his behavior was affecting them.

Sociopaths can't tolerate stability, and they sabotage it whenever they can. They thrive on chaos and danger—on living life at the edge of the cliff. They are rarely at rest, and deception and lying satisfy their virtually unquenchable need for stimulation.

I never knew for sure where he was or who he was with. One night he said he was going out for coffee, and when I offered to make some, he said he wanted to get some air. He was gone about two hours, but when I questioned him about it he just said he'd been out walking. Then he said, "Well, if you must know, I was with a client of mine. She was in a really bad place and needed some extra attention."

A few weeks later, after confiding in her husband what had happened, Michael's client reported his "extra attention"—which involved persuading her that having sex with him would lift her depression—to his licensing board. And when they started to investigate him, several other women came forward. It turned out he'd been sleeping with a lot of his clients. When I asked him if it was true he said, "Sure—it's really helping them. I can't believe they'd turn on me like this." He said he was pretty sure he could talk his way out of it, but even if they pulled his license, Karen had plenty of money and he could set up some kind of "alternative" counseling center. When I dared to suggest he'd really messed up this time, he got furious and stormed out.

The chaos of juggling two women wasn't enough, so Michael threw in sexual involvements with women he was supposed to be helping. He sabotaged his professional life, but he couldn't have cared less. There was always another con to pull and another woman to bail him out. Totally ruthless and exploitive in his treatment of anyone who was unlucky enough to be in his life, Michael created a world where chaos reigned supreme. And when Laurie had the temerity to question what he was doing, his charm turned to the one emotion sociopaths are capable of feeling—rage. How dare she not give him total adulation and suggest that any of this could have been his responsibility?

THE SEXUAL SOCIOPATH

Hank was a classic con man who swept women off their feet and then used them for financial gain. Michael was destructive and deceptive in both his professional and personal life. But some sociopathic personalities are able to maintain a responsible and even outstanding professional life while being totally ruthless in their personal relationships. It's as if they draw a dividing line down the center of their life, with the cognitive, intellectual part remaining stable but the emotional part in turmoil.

Obviously, if your lover is in and out of trouble with the law, dealing drugs, has a history of jumping from one job to the next, and is always in debt, it's fairly easy to recognize that something is very wrong. But what about the successful man, the good provider, the man who appears to be devoted to his family, the man whose worst legal trouble is a speeding ticket—who also cheats on you regularly with large numbers of women?

"I'm the only person you need to interview for your new book," said the lovely blond woman when I brought her in for her first appointment. Her name was Ruth and she had been referred by a mutual friend. At forty-seven, Ruth is an extremely successful entertainment attorney married to another partner in the same firm, who is also a highly respected lawyer. Craig had been married twice before, but Ruth believed that she was the woman who could make him happy. They frequently did lecture tours and seminars together, and with their two beautiful children, large home, and active social life, they looked to the outside world like a truly golden couple. Indeed they might have been, except that Ruth had recently found out about Craig's double life—and it was a story that could put Casanova to shame.

I want to give my marriage one last chance. I want to know I've done everything I can do, Ruth began tearfully. It all came unglued when I found a note from Tiffany's in the mail thanking Craig for the purchase of a two-thousand-dollar necklace for "his wife." At first he denied knowing anything about it and said they must have gotten their sales records mixed up. I told him I would call the store and get it straightened out, and he suddenly got very pale and said, "We need to talk." I knew from the tone of his voice something awful was about to happen. He confessed he'd been having a relationship with another part-ner's wife—her name is Sandy—for the last two years, but that it was absolutely over and the necklace was a kind of peace offering to her because she had gone ballistic when he told her the affair had to stop.

I thought I was going to have a heart attack right then and there. My first impulse was to tell him he had to leave, but then I thought, Take it easy, Ruth—don't throw the baby out with the bathwater. You're not the first woman to get cheated on and we can work this out. Plus he agreed to go to therapy with me and swore that he loved only me and begged me not to leave.

If this had been the whole story, it would have been bad enough. But by the end of the session, I had learned that Craig had bragged to his secretary that he'd cheated on his other wives with "at least twenty-five women." And in addition to the torrid affair with Sandy, Craig was also having an affair with his secretary, one of the paralegals in the office, and using this same secretary, who was infatuated with him, to schedule his various liaisons. He told each woman he was going to marry her. In fact, it was his secretary who finally told Ruth about the extent of Craig's sexual exploits. He acknowledged that her account was true, and also that he had not ended the affair with Sandy but was still seeing her regularly. I wondered what kind of vitamins he was taking.

In some ways the sexual sociopath is the most baffling of all. He is a man who lives not on the fringes of society but very much in the center of things. He is highly competent in some parts of his life, but profoundly ruthless in intimate relationships. Com-pulsive cheating is a central part of the sexual sociopath's rou-tine, but it may be the only part that's out of line. In a sense, he can be called a partial sociopath, because the other aspects of his life appear to be relatively stable. But the cheating catches him up in the thrill of doing something forbidden. He faces the con-stant risk of being caught in his perpetual web of lies, which pro-vides the danger and chaos he craves, but he knows he won't get arrested. It's easy to see that what he wants is not a close, loving relationship but people to manipulate and deceive.

Nora, the teacher you met in Chapter 2, lived uneasily with the humiliation of Allen's blatant affair with "CG"—until she realized that he was involved with another woman, as well. The shock woke her up, and she could see clearly how Allen tended to treat the women in his life, not like people, but simply as the objects that could help him act out his sexual compulsions:

I truly believe that for him to see an attractive woman and not take her to bed would be like anybody else seeing a ten-dollar bill on the sidewalk and not picking it up. It was that mechanical. And he had to do it.

Nora also came to some interesting conclusions about some of the motivations behind her husband's compulsive sexual cheating:

It was almost as if he wanted to get caught. If he didn't want me to find out, he could have been a lot more careful. He left a lot of traces. He's a psychological mystery to me. I think that maybe he wanted me to find out to punish me for not being as sexy and exciting as the women he was having affairs with. It was a very good way to stick a knife in me.

She could be right. We have no way of knowing all the motivations driving someone who acts out sexually with many partners, but often there seems to be an angry, punitive quality underneath his callous behavior. It is certainly degrading to all the women involved, who are objectified and discarded on a regular basis. And it is extremely cruel to his partner should she find out, as she usually does.

HOW DID HE GET THIS WAY?

We have a need to understand and make sense of our world, a need that is particularly urgent for the woman teetering on the edge or recognizing that she is involved with a man who is incapable of most normal human emotions. It is equally urgent for women like Diana and Laurie, who are recovering from such relationships.

People want neat, logical answers about what makes people tick. The reality is that human behavior in many cases defies simple explanations. As I've mentioned, logical explanations and the links between cause and effect are often blurry, and it's important to remember that the human personality is formed by many forces. Old Freudian theories attempted to explain all human behavior, no matter how bizarre, as being entirely the outcome of parenting and environment. This concept has been replaced by a far more comprehensive and realistic view of how people get to be the way they are, which takes into account that each individual not only grows up in a particular set of social conditions but also has distinctive genetic programming and unique circuitry.

Both of these elements come into play in theories about what goes into the making of a sociopath.

Internally, the sociopath appears to be wired differently from the rest of us. His inner world is like a Swiss cheese riddled with holes. Somehow it never came together to form a conscience. He may have been unable to bond with his parents because they were absent or abusive. He may have been overindulged and allowed to act on his impulses without coming into contact with the consequences. He may always have had a low tolerance for frustration. Any of these factors could play a role in the formation of an adult sociopath. But we also need to consider that brain chemistry, the result of genetic and temperamental predispositions, may be the area that will ultimately yield the most valuable clues to this behavior that seems to defy all explanation, logic, and reason. In other words, he may simply have been born that way. Did environment trigger something in the genes, or genes trigger a personality that a child's parents withdrew from? Some unfortunate combination of environment and genes is probably at the root of sociopathy.

THE ROMANCE OF THE MAN GONE WRONG

It's difficult to see past the sociopath's facade of charm and persuasiveness in part because our culture has long romanticized a lot of the sociopath's behavior. Movies and books abound with stories of charming con men, both real and fictional. These characters are usually portrayed as basically lovable and decent men gone astray because of unfortunate life circumstances, a terrible family situation, or an uncaring society. The consequences of their actions have always been overshadowed by their romantic aura.

Laurie first saw her sociopathic boyfriend, Michael, as a wonderful guy who was the victim of a crazy family that was rife with dark secrets and lies:

One of his sisters told me that both she and another sister had been molested by their grandfather, and she suspects that Michael may have been molested as well. In addition, there's an uncle who is very physically inappropriate with his daughter. Everyone in the family is aware of the incest, but nobody does anything about it. Plus everybody is either alcoholic, a druggie, or abusive. So how could he be healthy coming from this background? But I thought he had a good heart—he was a therapist, after all—and he was really the sane one. Who could blame him for being a little difficult sometimes?

Michael's family gave new meaning to the overused term *dysfunctional*. Anyone growing up in a family with this much pathology is going to have enormous problems, but who knows why someone else from the same family might have turned out to be a troubled but responsible adult and Michael turned out to be a chronic liar and sexual addict without conscience? It's true that Michael had a lot going against him, but that in no way justifies the way he chose to live his life, though Laurie clung to the romantic notion that it did.

THE $64,000 QUESTION: CAN HE CHANGE?

"If only he'd get some help," the partner of the sociopath says wistfully.

I'm sympathetic, but I know I have to dash her hopes by answering, "It won't do any good."

Unlike the neurotic, or even psychotic, for whom many effective treatment methods have been developed, the sociopath is in a totally different diagnostic category. He is personality and character disordered. That means he has deeply ingrained flaws in his basic character structure, which rarely, if ever, yield to any current interventions.

Traditional therapy is totally ineffective with the sociopath because he lacks the crucial internal elements needed to have any kind of successful therapeutic experience:

1. He doesn't experience the pain that motivates people to change.
2. He doesn't believe that what he's done is wrong.
3. He has no access to his emotional self.
4. He is without the moral and ethical borders that would create feelings of guilt or shame about his behavior.
5. He thinks he's smarter than everyone else.
6. He will come into therapy only because he's been ordered there by a judge or to placate a partner he's not ready to discard. He will not stay long.
7. He won't tell the truth and is often very successful at conning the therapist.

On the rare occasions when a sociopath does come in to see a therapist because it's in his best interests to do so, he'll spend a lot of time trying to convince his partner and the therapist that he realizes his mistakes.

Nora clung to the small hope that therapy could repair her marriage, although I told her I didn't feel very optimistic about the outcome. She told Allen she'd give him one last chance if he'd come in with her to see me—otherwise, she'd go by herself to see a divorce lawyer. Allen showed up all right, but he acted like a kid who'd been caught stealing candy instead of a man who had caused enormous heartache. When I tried to find out if he had any idea how damaging his cheating had been, the dialogue went like this:

Susan: Do you have any sense of how your behavior has made your wife feel?

Allen: Oh, absolutely. I hurt the one person in the world that means everything to me. All I'm asking for is one more chance to prove that I can change. I'm not a bad guy—honest. Those other women didn't mean anything to me.

Susan: And what kind of changes do you need to make?

Allen: Well, obviously, I have to keep my zipper closed and have some willpower.

Nora: So how do you think that's going to happen? You've made a lot of promises in the past, but you didn't keep any of them.

Allen: Well, give me a break here—I mean I'll just have to work at it, and it'll take some time, but I know I can do it if you'll give me a chance. Honey, you have to believe me, I never wanted to destroy the marriage.

Susan: There have been some strong indications that some of the new medications are very useful in controlling impulsive sexual acting out.

Allen: I would never consider anything like that. I thought we were here to talk about saving our marriage. I'm all for talking to somebody from time to time. I've got a really busy schedule so it can't be on a regular basis, but hey—I'm going to give this a hundred percent.

Allen was all false repentance, even managed to shed a few tears as he asked his wife for patience and forgiveness and assured her that he would change. He took no responsibility for his behavior and even made light of it. When backed into a corner about making a commitment to any kind of help, he was evasive.

Sociopaths do not learn from experience, or even from punishment. If they lose a relationship, there's always another one waiting in the wings. Nothing will keep them from reverting to their destructive behavior.

Three weeks after this session, Nora told me sadly that she had filed for divorce.

There was a little window of time where he seemed to be straightening out and I really had some hope, but two days ago he took off for a weekend with someone and didn't even bother to lie about it!

Anyone who says it's possible to make a relationship with a sociopath work is either ignorant or lying. Of course the person most likely to say this is the sociopath himself. The sad truth is, Nora would have been better off with a heroin addict. At least some of them can be helped.

SOLO SURVIVAL

For almost every woman involved with a sociopath, there comes a moment when she recognizes that she cannot continue to be his partner in deceit. Sometimes it happens quite suddenly, when one event triggers a final crisis. It can be the discovery of a depleted bank account, a foreclosure notice served on a mortgage he swore he was taking care of, learning of yet another affair after he's promised to be faithful, or a discovery of illegal activities.

This chapter is not about repairing a damaged relationship, it's about saving the one person who's salvageable—you. At the beginning of this chapter, I told you that there is one type of man you must leave, and now you know a lot more about why this is so. With the emerging recognition of what has happened, it's perfectly natural to have feelings of self-reproach and humiliation. In the second half of this book, I will help you pick up the pieces, and together we will build a bridge to take you from this deeply painful emotional spot to the other side of the abyss.

5

The Lies Women Tell Themselves

When your lover is a liar, you and he have a lot in common—you're both lying to you.

It's not hard to see why women so readily comfort themselves with lies when truth and trust begin to disappear in a relationship. None of us wants to face the fact of a lover's lying, and to avoid that pain, most of us resort to the very same defenses our lovers use—and for surprisingly similar reasons. He uses denial to keep the truth from you. You use denial to keep the truth from yourself as well. When his lies are discovered, he rationalizes to justify his lying. And so do you.

By lying to yourself, you play a subtle but crucial role in perpetuating your lover's deceptions. You may believe that your role is fairly passive—after all, you're the one who's been on the receiving end of his lies, not the one who's engineered the betrayal. But in the name of love, trust, saving the relationship, and a dozen other wonderful-sounding ideals, you may quietly provide the signals that let your lover know the lying can continue. All you have to do is look the other way or pretend everything's OK. It's easy. Just as many seemingly great guys are great liars, many otherwise smart women are great pretenders. In this chapter, I'll help you cut through the falsehoods that help women perpetuate men's lying. Get ready for a reality check.

DENIAL: BLIND FAITH

Denial, as most of you know by now, is the see-no-evil, hear-no-evil, speak-no-evil way of avoiding facts that may be deeply troubling. We frequently ignore clear evidence, deflect the truth, and find ways to block out all the inner voices that warn us something's wrong.

We cling to erroneous assumptions about our men and our relationships, unwilling to update them based on new information. We trust—because we trust. We decide that he's not the kind of man who would (pick one) lie about money/drink/gamble/cheat on me/hide things from me—and that's that. All signs to the contrary get discarded because they don't fit the reality we've eagerly embraced. So the first hurdle a lie has to pass before it enters our consciousness is a belief, almost impenetrable in some women, that says, "It can't be happening because it can't happen to me."

SELF-LIE NO. 1: HE WOULD NEVER LIE TO ME

Many a woman believes that because she is in an intimate relationship, she really knows her partner well. She's convinced that there's no way he could hide a lie—or want to—and if you asked her how she knew, she'd probably answer, "Because I know how he ticks. He's just not capable of lying to me." Or "I just know." Or "Because he told me he would never lie to me, and I believe him." In some cases she will be right. But it's not unlikely that she will be very wrong. Kathy was in the second category.

As Kathy looked back on the early days of her relationship with David, she saw how many false assumptions she'd made about him based on his behavior in a controlled, structured situation: their AA meetings. She didn't realize how little she knew about his behavior in the rest of his life, or how different it might be:

I thought I really understood him. He was so open and forthcoming in our meetings, I thought I knew him to the core. There's such a premium on honesty and personal responsibility

*in this work that from the beginning I truly believed that lying
would be as odious to him as it was to me—that he would never
lie to me. If I had it to do over again, I would have waited
longer to move in with him. I thought I was being careful, but I
just didn't have enough information, and once I decided I could
trust him, I took his word about everything. I gave my trust
away too quickly.*

If you are basically honest, especially about the important
things, you will tend to project those qualities onto other people
and assume that they are going to think, feel, and behave the way
you do. Kathy ascribed much of her own character and values to
David and assumed he shared them. And he did—at meetings.
But once they entered into an intimate relationship, his behavior
became dramatically different.

No Experience with Betrayal

For Anne, it was natural to assume the best because she'd been
fortunate enough to be able to do that in the past.

*I grew up in a wonderful family. I guess in some ways you
could say I had a very sheltered life. I had two parents who loved
each other and were absolutely terrific to my brother and me. I
know it sounds too good to be true, but honestly, all I knew was
love and trust. I had no experience with betrayal—it wasn't in
my frame of reference. When I married Randy I just assumed it
would be a continuation of what I knew growing up. I truly
believed he would never lie to me about anything important. I
feel like something in me died—all that wonderful innocence. . . .*

Trust was something that came easily and naturally to Anne
because it was familiar to her—it was what she had seen at home
and had come to expect. It was as though what was happening to
her had no way to fit into her belief system. And now that she'd
been faced with a wrenching betrayal, she had to find a way to
make sense of the world.

As Kathy discovered, you don't really know any man until you
have been in a relationship with him for a significant time. And

even then, when questions arise about his behavior, they often go unasked. It's very important for most women to look loving and trusting, believing that a little skepticism, even in the face of evidence that all is not on the up-and-up, has no place in a love relationship. And some, like Anne, don't pick up clues because they just don't believe it's necessary to look.

Reality Check

Don't assume—gather information. You don't need to shut off your brain just because your heart is involved. Remember: It is behind the front door that people's dark sides will emerge. Intimate relationships activate our insecurities and anxieties, and a man may be very different in situations with other people than he is with you. Sometimes the biggest lie a man will tell you is "I would never lie to you." To really know somebody takes time—months, not moments. Trust has to be earned. Don't give it away prematurely or go through your relationship in a state of oblivion.

SELF-LIE NO. 2: MAYBE HE'S LIED TO OTHER WOMEN, BUT HE WON'T LIE TO ME

When I first started working with Allison, she wouldn't even consider the possibility that Scott might have lied to her. Although some of his friends had been fairly open about his womanizing in his previous marriage, and even kidded about it in front of her, she wasn't particularly concerned about it. After all, his first wife had been such a bitch that anybody would have turned to other women. And how did she know so much about his ex? Scott had told her, of course—just as he'd told her so convincingly about helping an alcoholic friend on the night her sister, Erica, saw him with a woman in a bar.

Allison believed that what she and Scott had was so special, he couldn't possibly want or need anything or anyone else. And much of that belief was propelled by the intensity of their sexual relationship:

There's no way he would ever be unfaithful to me, because he loves me and we have such great sex. I don't know too many couples who've been together as long as we have who just can't keep their hands off each other. That's not something you can fake. So why would he need to see another woman? Or to put it in his words, "Why go out for a sandwich when you have a Roman banquet at home?" When he says, "I love you," I know he means it. The proof is in the bedroom, the kitchen, the front seat of the car—if that's not love, I don't know what is.

What it is is wonderful, passionate, exciting sex, which can easily obscure other facets of a relationship—such little things as honesty, respect, fidelity, and character. There are few things more bewildering to a woman than discovering her lover has cheated on her when the sex is so terrific.

Reality Check
Great sex doesn't always equal fidelity. The old cliché that men cheat on their wives because they are dissatisfied sexually is true in some cases and not true in many others. As Allison later discovered, many men are able to have an intense sexual relationship with their partner and still pick up a woman in a bar or at a convention or on an out-of-town business trip and have a quick fling. Some men can carry on a passionate sexual relationship with their wives and one or more mistresses. Most women equate lovemaking with love. But contrary to what most women would like to believe, for some men there's little correlation between the two.

"THIS TIME IT'S DIFFERENT"
A woman who's involved with a married man is automatically involved with a man who lies—it's built into the situation because he is most certainly lying to his wife. Almost every woman who's in love with such a man tells herself, and anybody else who will listen, that her situation is unique—that he doesn't lie to her, and he *will* leave his wife.

In our first session, Natalie, a thirty-eight-year-old executive secretary, told me an all too familiar story of a long-term affair with a married man—one that started out passionately and full of excitement. Now it was creating enormous anxiety and uncertainty for her.

I had a terrible marriage, and I was yearning for someone to make me feel attractive and desirable, and Larry does that in spades. He's a forensic accountant, so he was able to see me a lot at night and tell his wife he was working. I know that he's lying to her, but it's the only way we can be together right now, and because what we have is so special, I know he would never lie to me. Of course, there are a lot of drawbacks. At first I accepted the limits, but weekends and holidays were lonely. I want more. I want to be his wife. He told me that he was devoted to his kids but that the marriage was dead emotionally and sexually. That makes me feel less guilty about what we're doing and about wanting him to marry me.

In just a few minutes, Natalie had described several of the elements that are almost always part of a relationship with a married man:

1. He insists that he and his wife don't love each other anymore and they don't have sex.
2. He tells his wife he's working when he's seeing his lover.
3. He will not be with this lover on weekends or holidays. He will be with his family. She probably doesn't even go out with friends at those times because she doesn't want to miss the call he makes when his wife goes out for a while.

BELIEVING WHAT HE SAYS, NOT WHAT HE DOES

Natalie wanted so much to believe that Larry would leave his wife and be with her that she focused almost exclusively on his words rather than his actions. His words told her what she wanted to hear, and gave her hope to cling to. His behavior, though, told a different story, which she let blur into the background.

When I pressed him, he made promises: "I can't imagine my life without you. We'll be together, we'll have a life together." I wanted to believe, even when he came up with the standard married man evasion—"When the kids are older, I'll get a divorce." I kept asking him to give me some indication of how much time he thought it would take before he could leave, and he would say, "I can't give you a date yet, but trust me, it will happen." This went on for four years, and I finally gave him an ultimatum. I wouldn't go on. So last night, under pressure from me, he said he would move out and rent an apartment. I'm thrilled. I'm scared. I'm confused. I don't know if I'm doing the right thing or not.

BE CAREFUL WHAT YOU WISH FOR

I told Natalie that as I listened to her, I had the same kind of foreboding I have when I watch a scary movie where a woman is in the house at night and hears a noise down in the basement. Alone, and with no light, she goes down to check it out. As she starts down the stairs, I always find myself thinking, "No! Don't do it—go back—it's not safe!"

Disaster was just around the corner for Natalie, not in the form of a horror movie surprise, but in the face of an exciting man who was promising her everything she thought she wanted. Unfortunately, she and Larry were both lying to her. When I saw Natalie the following week, her demeanor was very different. As she told me what had happened, her story was punctuated with tears and feelings of bewilderment.

We made a date for ten in the morning to meet at a real estate office and look for a house for him to rent. Naturally, I got there fifteen minutes early. And I waited . . . and waited. I guess I sat there for over an hour and a half. People were asking me if they could help me and I kept saying, "No, I'm waiting for someone." I read every magazine they had. First I wondered if something had happened to him, but then I realized that he just wasn't going to show up . . . that this wasn't going to happen. I felt sick to my stomach. This couldn't be happening.

The shock and disbelief that Natalie described are familiar to anyone who's ever had a dream die. To add to her humiliation and sense of betrayal, Larry didn't even have the guts to face her.

I called him at his office and he wouldn't take my call. In fact, he wouldn't take my calls for a week. When he finally did, he said, "I'm so sorry, but I just can't do this now." And that was pretty much it.

Natalie's once passionate affair ended with a whimper. No big dramatic scene. Just a feeble "I'm sorry" and the click of a telephone being hung up.

Reality Check
If your lover lies to his wife, chances are pretty good that he's lying to you as well. Larry never had any intention of leaving. His promises of a future were his way of keeping Natalie hooked in. Like most married men, he wanted it all—the wife, the kids, the house, and his lover. When Natalie rocked his boat, he jumped ship.

Certainly some married men do leave their wives for their lovers, and I know of a few good relationships that came out of circumstances like that. But those situations are very much in the minority, and the odds of it happening if you continue in a long-term affair with him are not weighted in your favor. Even if he should leave, what makes you think he won't ultimately do the same thing to you?

MAKING THE LIE MAKE SENSE

When denial (his or ours) can no longer hold and we finally have to admit to ourselves that we've been lied to, we search frantically for ways to keep it from disrupting our lives. So we rationalize. We find "good reasons" to justify his lying, just as he almost always accompanies his confessions with "good reasons" for his lies. He tells us he only lied because.... We tell ourselves he only lied because.... We make excuses for him:

The lying wasn't significant/Everybody lies/He's only human/I have no right to judge him.

Allowing the lies to register in our consciousness means having to make room for any number of frightening possibilities:

- He's not the man I thought he was.
- The relationship has spun out of control and I don't know what to do.
- The relationship may be over.

Most women will do almost anything to avoid having to face these truths. Even if we yell and scream at him when we discover that he's lied to us, once the dust settles, most of us will opt for the comforting territory of rationalization. In fact, many of us are willing to rewire our senses, short-circuit our instincts and intelligence, and accept the seductive comfort of self-delusion.

But we're not stupid. Our rationalizations have to make sense to us or they just won't work. If yours are so precious that you can't go on without them, stop reading now. I'm about to punch some holes in the rationalizations that may be keeping you from taking effective action, and once they've been punctured, they will never work as well again.

SELF-LIE NO. 3: YES, HE LIES, BUT HE LOVES ME AND THAT'S ALL THAT MATTERS

Many women are so hungry for love and emotional security that they forget how love is supposed to feel and that sometimes the words "I love you" can be a lie as well. That reality becomes very clear when we look at how easy it is for some of the women we've already met to overvalue the words "I love you" when their partners are being anything but loving:

- Jan believes that Bill's failure to tell her about his second marriage proves how much he loves her. Why? Because he says so. "He only lied to me because he was afraid that if I knew about Carla I'd reject him. You don't know how touching it was to hear him say, 'I was afraid I'd lose you.'"

- Kathy sees David as her best friend and the love of her life, even when he threatens her financial security, undermines her confidence, and breaks the promise that was such a fundamental part of their relationship—that he would stay sober. Why? Because he apologizes and says, "I love you."
- Natalie endures four years of loneliness and frustration with her married lover. Why? Because he says, "I love you," and promises that they'll have a life together.
- Carol takes Ken back repeatedly, even after he abuses her. Why? "He's so sincere and remorseful—so afraid of losing me. I know he has this really dark part, but I can also see the good in him. I can see the love in his eyes when he says, 'I love you.'"

DEFINING LOVE

If you asked any of the men you've met so far in this book whether they loved their partners, the answer would undoubtedly have been "Of course." And most of them, sociopaths excepted, would genuinely believe what they were saying. But in order to really understand what they mean by love, it's crucial to look at what they're doing.

Love has dozens of meanings, depending on who's describing it. It's a combination of subjective feelings of pleasure in another's company, attraction, need, desire, and sexual passion. Certainly many of the men we've met feel some or all of those things. But those feelings are not enough to define genuine love. Feelings must also translate to a way of treating the other person—to actively nurturing the partner's emotional and spiritual well-being. Love doesn't betray and deceive. Love doesn't make you feel stupid and enraged and tricked. Without loving behavior, love becomes an empty word used far too often by men who lie to assuage their partner's anger or suspicions.

Reality Check

Love is a verb, not a noun. It is active. Love is not just feelings of passion and romance. It is behavior. If a man lies to you, he is behaving badly and unlovingly

*toward you. He is disrespecting you and your relation-
ship. The words "I love you" are not enough to make up
for that. Don't kid yourself that they are.*

SELF-LIE NO. 4: YES, HE LIES, BUT HE'S A VICTIM OF CIRCUMSTANCES

The poor guy! He only lies because he had a terrible childhood/his
mother died when he was eight/his father was an alcoholic/his
parents had no money when he was small and the kids made fun
of his thrift-shop clothes/his boss is a jerk and he's under terrible
pressure at work/his ex-wife is a total bitch and she's still making
his life miserable. Of course he lies! Who wouldn't with that many
problems?

What you've just read is a litany of misplaced compassion. In
the name of empathy, it's easy for many women to open their
hearts and gloss over repeated lying, even when it's profoundly
damaging to them. Coached by a man who lies, they can detail
the traumas and pressures—both old and current—that he's
under and work them around to justify his lies. These woman
become far more adept at protecting him than themselves.

Diane, the paralegal, is very vulnerable to seeing the lying of
her husband, Ben, as an understandable outgrowth of tough circumstances:

*His parents split up right after he was born, and he was
raised by his grandparents, who were very poor. He doesn't
keep any pictures of his family around because I think it's too
painful for him. And I really understand that—my family was
no Brady Bunch. So it's amazing how far he's come. And I
understand totally why he feels he has to do so much for
Peggy—he wants to be the good dad he never had. And if he
exaggerates to look like a big shot and he lets off a little steam
once in a while . . . well, it's tough out there. I just wish he'd
level with me a little more.*

Compassion is wonderful, and so is being supportive, but
Diane is turning those qualities into the stuff of self-delusion. Her

sympathy for Ben's past and present difficulties overrides her anger at being deceived. She labels his unhealthy behavior in benign terms—his yelling at her when she attempts to talk to him about money becomes "letting off a little steam." If she stopped rationalizing, though, she would have to face the fact that he has lied to her repeatedly, has spent a great deal of their money on speculative schemes without telling her about it, and takes no responsibility for the serious financial crisis they're in. She would also have to take some action on her own behalf—something a lot of women are eager to avoid. Instead, she passively wishes that Ben would "level with her a little more." Wishing, however, will not make everything magically change.

For some women there's nothing more satisfying than being a supportive partner to a man who's had a hard time in his life and is struggling, especially if they've had a difficult childhood or adolescence themselves.

It didn't surprise me to learn that Diane had been consistently physically and verbally abused as a child by her mother. She overidentified with Ben's difficulties and offered him the caring and compassion she told me she had always yearned for. By being so understanding and so forgiving with Ben, she was really treating him the way she would have wanted to be treated, and was vicariously nurturing herself as well. But while playing Saint Diane, she was also creating the perfect climate for Ben to continue doing exactly what he was doing.

Reality Check

Many people had tough childhoods, and they don't lie repeatedly. Lying to you won't change his childhood, and constantly forgiving him won't change yours. It won't relieve stress or pressure—it just creates more. It won't improve his self-image. Understanding and forgiveness without effective action only give him further permission to lie to you because lying doesn't cost him anything. It would be nice if Diane could spread some of that ready compassion around to include herself.

SELF-LIE NO. 5: YES, HE LIES, BUT I CAN FIX HIM

Closely connected to "Yes, he lies, but it's because of all the bad things that have happened to him" is a self-lie that goes "Yes, he lies, but I can change him."

Some women see their lover's lying as a challenge. They're disturbed but undaunted when lies begin to crop up because they're sure they have all the love and skills they need to set an errant lover back on the right track. They are in love with the person they know he could be.

Kathy labored under this belief:

I would say to him, "Tell me the truth. Let's clear the air." See—I always felt I could control things and make them better. I've always been the family mediator, therapist, healer. I'm fantastic with the patients at the hospital, so surely I can help someone I love. I couldn't believe I could be defeated by his lying. I always believed if I did A-B-C, then D-E-F would have to follow . . . but it didn't. I got so fed up with coming home and not knowing what I'd find.

Kathy grew up in an unstable family. Her parents divorced when she was ten, and her mother began drinking heavily. Kathy, like so many children of alcoholic parents, became her mother's caretaker—the one who ran the household when her mother was too drunk to function. Although she was deprived of many normal childhood activities, there was also a payoff for her in this unfortunate role reversal: Kathy was lauded by her mother and other family members for her maturity and self-sacrifice. It became an important part of her identity and strongly influenced her choice of profession.

A great deal of Kathy's self-image is tied up in her role of mediator and healer. As a nurse, she's seen how her talents have worked real changes in people's lives, and that gives her the confidence that she can bring the same skills to bear in her marriage. But David is a different story. He's a great talker, and he knows how to play the "Let's talk things out" game without making any actual changes. All he has to do is say, "I've seen the error of my ways," and Kathy thinks she's fixed him—he's seen the light.

Fixers assume that because they're grown-up they will be able to do with their lovers what they couldn't do for their parents when they were little. But Kathy is no more able to fix David than she was able to change her mother.

Reality Check

When we want desperately to preserve a relationship, we will zero in on anything our partner may say that gives us hope that he will change. But words are just words, and as Kathy found, unless they're backed up by action, they have about as much meaning as gibberish.

The only one who can fix, rescue, or change your lover is himself. The ball has to be placed squarely in his court. You may be smart, effective, even powerful, but nobody is powerful enough to change another person's nature.

SELF-LIE NO. 6: YES, HE LIES, BUT IT'S MY FAULT

It's often difficult for a woman to connect lying with the man she loves. If he really betrayed her the way her gut tells her he did, the pain of knowing that dark side of him would be horrendous. As her mind frantically searches for a more acceptable way of making sense of what is happening, she often seizes on an insidious, though comforting, line of reasoning: "It must have been my fault." And once a woman falls into the trap of blaming herself for her lover's lies, she embarks on a path of clouded perceptions and distorted reality.

When David told Kathy that he'd fallen off the wagon because of her, everything she had learned about personal responsibility in AA went temporarily out the window:

Maybe he's right—maybe I did let him down and didn't give him enough warning about leaving. I probably could have handled it a lot better. . . . He needs me so much and I should have stayed and worked things out with him. . . . Maybe I really did cause him to start drinking again.

It may be hard to understand why it would be more self-protective for Kathy to blame herself for his lies than to put the responsibility where it belongs, but unfortunately, many women willingly heap ashes on their own heads if it allows them to continue in their relationship.

Kathy was trying to convince herself—and me—that David started drinking again because she was a bad wife who cruelly and thoughtlessly left her husband. This familiar "should have, could have" speculating is what a lot of women do to convince themselves that he's OK and she's the one at fault because she didn't handle things right. "Maybe I should have done this instead of that," they reason, or "Maybe I zigged when I should have zagged." Kathy's need to absolve David of any responsibility for his choices overpowered the fact that she left him because his behavior was becoming so unpredictable and frightening.

Other familiar self-blaming rationalizations sound like this:

- He only lied because I'm too controlling.
- He only lied because I can't handle problems well.
- He only lied because I'm so insecure—he really did it to protect me.
- He only had an affair because I'm too fat/too thin/not supportive enough/not exciting enough/I don't give him enough sex/I'm too critical/I'm a nag/I complain too much.

You probably have plenty of your own to add to the list.

SELF-BLAME AND DEPENDENCY

Even though Kathy was competent and independent in many areas of her life, she was very emotionally dependent on David and his close-knit family:

I enjoy being married. I don't want to be single again. I don't want to lose the family—especially his mother. She and I are closer than I ever was with my own mother. I'll do anything to hold on to that.

Including blaming herself for David's lies.

To help her figure out why she was turning reality upside-down, I asked Kathy to think of a small child whose parent or parents are behaving hurtfully toward her. In order to survive emotionally, that child develops powerful means to avoid seeing her parents as bad in any way. If she allowed the truth of their behavior to get through her defenses, she would feel unbearable anxiety because she is totally dependent on them. And if they're truly bad, she might not survive. Therefore she must see them as good. So the child reasons this way: "If I feel bad, or bad things are happening to me, it must be because I am bad." By making herself the cause of what is being done to her, the child brings order to a chaotic universe. It's far less terrifying for her to believe that she is bad than to acknowledge the harmful intent of those powerful, big people she needs so desperately.

For many women, the willingness to believe that they are to blame for their partner's lies is often a direct replay in adult life of this early attempt at psychological survival. When you layer onto that the accusations from your partner—claims that he only lied to you because of some deficiency in you—self-blame can easily become an integral part of how you define what's going on between you.

If you acknowledge to yourself that he's the one who's done something very wrong, then your world is not a safe place, and everything you thought you could count on starts to crumble. But if you blame yourself, then your energies can go into fixing your deficiencies and continuing to collude with your partner in shifting the responsibility for his behavior onto you.

HIS LIES, YOUR COLLUSION

Nora was furious at Allen's repetitive betrayals, but she still viewed herself as the problem that caused him to lie to her. As a result, she bought his attacks on her sexuality without even questioning their validity.

> *I tried to do a lot of rationalizing to make myself feel better—things like "I'm no good in bed—if I were more exciting, he wouldn't have to look elsewhere. . . ." And you know, I had a small child and I was tired a lot of the time, and I'll admit I didn't always feel very sexy, but I guess I should have faked it.*

By blaming herself for Allen's compulsive womanizing, Nora was colluding with Allen in a way that gave him license to indulge in his sexual addiction, just as Kathy's colluding with David allowed him to continue drinking and being irresponsible with money.

If Allen was unhappy with his and Nora's sexual relationship, there were many options available other than lying and sleeping with as many women as he could. I asked Nora if she ever stopped blaming herself for Allen's behavior long enough to consider that Allen might be a lousy lover. Compulsive womanizers frequently are, because sex is rarely an act of love for them but rather an outlet to alleviate pressure and anxiety. Nora may have had some sexual problems of her own, but Allen's sexual problems were far more serious, destructive, and in today's reality, downright dangerous.

Collusion is a dangerous dynamic in a relationship with a man who lies. It means that you have become a participant in his lying. It means that you have renounced your right to define reality and accepted his version of what is happening. When that version focuses on how some flaw in you caused him to lie, and you accept that as truth, you are actually aiding and abetting his lying.

Reality Check

His lying is not contingent on who you are or what you do. His lying is not your fault. Lying is his choice and his problem, and if he makes that choice with you, he will make it with any other woman he's with. That doesn't mean you're an angel and he's the devil. It does mean that if he doesn't like certain things about you, he has many ways to address them besides lying. If there are sexual problems between you, there are many resources available to help you. Nothing can change until you hold him responsible and accountable for lying and stop blaming yourself.

The lies we tell ourselves to keep from seeing the truth about our lovers don't feel like lies. They feel comfortable, familiar, and true. We repeat them like a mantra and cling to them like security blankets, hoping to calm ourselves and regain our sense that the world works the way we believe it ought to.

Self-lies are false friends we look to for comfort and protection—and for a short time they may make us feel better. But we can only keep the truth at bay for so long. Our self-lies can't erase his lies, and as we'll see, the longer we try to pretend they can, the more we deepen the hurt.

6

What Lying Does to Us

Living with our lover's lies changes us at the very core of our being. It affects our thoughts, our feelings, our behavior, our relationships with the other people in our lives—and our self-respect. The changes may begin with the lies we tell ourselves to blunt our suspicions and fears, or with the accommodations we make to adjust to living with lies. But just as surely as a trickle of water will eventually wear away even the hardest granite, the choices we make to deny or soften the pain of his lying eat steadily away at the very foundation of our well-being.

We become depressed. We want to retaliate. We no longer know the person we love, and we no longer know ourselves. We adopt behaviors that we'd reject in any other circumstances and become locked in a war between our most powerful emotions. Whether we acknowledge it or not, we're barraged with self-contempt. We feel stupid, used, tricked, ashamed.

The roar of negative thoughts and painful feelings within usually seems to us to be the most direct effect of our partner's lying, and it's the one we often pay the most attention to. Distracted by the very real drama of our anger and grief, we may barely notice the other significant changes that are taking place in our lives. These changes may not happen overnight, but they are definitely part of the fallout of living with deception.

As a result of his lies, you may:

- Cut yourself off from people close to you who know he's lying
- Become a partner in his lying to protect him
- Attempt to get revenge through impulsive retaliatory actions
- Find yourself so jealous and suspicious that you humiliate and degrade yourself
- Become bitter and walled-off
- Become increasingly tolerant of lying
- Imprint your children with the message that men are allowed to lie and women are supposed to put up with it

No one sets out purposely to do any of these things. But if we continue to be reactive rather than proactive in the face of our lover's lies, we often lose the best parts of ourselves. Let's look in detail at how that happens.

OUR LOVER LIES, WE KILL THE MESSENGER

For hundreds of years, news was carried by way of messenger. When the news was good, the messenger was rewarded. But often these poor souls found themselves in the difficult position of having to relay bad news to a king or other powerful person. Hearing the details of unpleasant or tragic events like death, the loss of a major battle or war, plots against the crown, or various forms of treachery and betrayal, the king would become enraged—and look for a scapegoat to blame for his misery. Who better than the person he saw as the cause of his distress: the messenger. If not for him, the king would still be ignorant of these unhappy events and could continue his normal routine. What better solution, then, than banishing the bearer of ill tidings—or putting him to death?

The idea of killing the messenger didn't disappear with modern technology. In a figurative sense, it is very much a part of contemporary life. We are still far more likely to get angry at the person who tells us bad news than at the person who created the problem.

Allison responded dramatically when her sister, Erica, mentioned seeing Scott leaving a bar with another woman:

I called Erica the next day and told her that she should mind her own business. I said she must have seen someone who looked like Scott. She said she was sitting quite near him even though he didn't see her, and there was no mistake. Then she said, "Honey—how much longer are you going to let him do this to you?" I just lost it. I screamed at her: "You don't know anything about what we have together. How dare you try to break up my marriage." I told her I didn't want to see her or hear from her until she apologized to me. I mean, here she's supposed to be my best friend, and she was attacking Scott and hitting me where it really hurt. I really felt she betrayed me.

For women like Allison with strong denial systems, it's essential to block out even the most glaring signs that lies are beginning to overshadow the relationship.

With rose-colored glasses firmly in place, she could make the most blatant lie disappear. Erica truly cared about her sister, and lacking Allison's customized filters for interpreting Scott's actions, she was far more able to see his lies for what they really were.

But this put Erica in an untenable position. Should she keep quiet and hope Allison would ultimately find out the truth for herself? Or should she risk incurring Allison's enmity by becoming the modern-day equivalent of the messenger who brings news no one wants to hear? It's a dilemma that anyone who genuinely cares about us struggles with when they try to protect us or wake us up to what's happening in our lives. And the stronger our denial, the less we want anyone to pierce it. As a result, we often cut ourselves off from important people who are telling us things we may not be ready to hear.

The intensity of Allison's defensiveness was a strong indication that she was beginning to have some real doubts about who was being straight with her. But sometimes, even as the truth is beginning to permeate, when we hear it from someone else it feels almost like an assault. It was easier for Allison to feel betrayed by her sister, who was telling her the truth, than to face the possibility that Scott was the one who was doing the betraying. And just as the king would displace his anger onto the messenger, Allison displaced hers onto Erica.

Us Against Them

In Diane's case, it was her mother who was temporarily banished. Diane was fully aware of Ben's lies about his business deals and their very precarious financial situation, but she didn't want to hear about them from anyone else. She didn't want to lose hope.

I was living on promises, and it was getting harder and harder. My mom had this annoying habit of interrogating me about what was going on—I know she was worried about me— so I told her about this very important project he was working on—one that he assured me would give us total financial security. I think I was trying to reassure myself as well as her. She was quiet for a minute and then she said, "But I've been hearing about this for over a year now." She said that she and my dad had asked some real estate people about this particular project, and they had said that Ben wouldn't be able to get the zoning he needed and that several other big developers had walked away from it for that reason. Ben had told me the zoning was just about set. Then she said, "Just tell me the truth—is he making any money at all, or are you supporting him?" It was just one question, but I heard it as an indictment of my judgment, my life, my marriage. I felt so raw—all my nerve ends were ragged—I couldn't think straight. Why did my mother need to do this to me? I told her I couldn't talk anymore and not to call me until she was ready to show some respect to my husband.

When you're living with escalating chaos and trying to convince those around you that everything is, or will be, fine, you often demand that others either go along with your self-delusions or stay away. You don't want outside reality checks to interfere with the false reality you've created for yourself, so you often stop opening up to the people you've been close to—or sometimes stop seeing them altogether. The only people you feel comfortable with are those who will tell you what you want to hear.

Even if you continue to see certain friends or family members, you stop sharing your concerns or asking for their take on what's happening. You tell yourself that no one understands what's going on. No one knows him the way you do. You start to keep secrets.

The more you hide, the less truth and intimacy you allow. Embarrassment, defensiveness, and anger fill the space that used to be full of closeness. Anyone who won't go along with your self-lies may suddenly find they have no place in your life.

I'm not suggesting that you tolerate meddling or snooping from anyone. And I'm certainly not suggesting that you automatically believe everything anyone tells you. We all know that some people in our lives have less than pure motives and agendas. But if the messenger has been trustworthy in the past, you owe it to yourself to at least check out what they're telling you, no matter how frightening it may be. This is not disloyalty—it's self-preservation.

LYING BY PROXY

It's not unusual for a man who lies to enlist his partner in the juggling act he uses to stay one step ahead of the consequences. This is especially true when his lies are about money, missing work, or addiction. Caught in a no-win situation, you may knowingly, though unwillingly, become complicit in his lies.

Diane told me that it became her job to deal with creditors because Ben had stalled them for so long with promises of payments which never materialized that no one believed him anymore:

When the walls started closing in on us, he would have me intervene with the people we owed money to. It was "Tell them I'm not here" when he was, or "Tell them I sent the check" when he hadn't, or "Tell them I'll call them back." So now I'm lying for him, which I hated. But he convinced me that I could buy us more time than he could because people are usually more sympathetic to a woman. A couple of times I broke down and cried on the telephone—I felt so degraded, so tacky.

The less credibility your lover has, the more he needs yours. Before you know it, you may find yourself lying not only to strangers, but to people you care about as well.

Diane panicked when she got a foreclosure notice from the

savings and loan that held the mortgage on their home, a few months after she discovered that Ben had been stashing the payment notices in the desk:

> *I couldn't believe how casual he could be about it. He said, "Your mother's loaded—she can help us out till that Santa Barbara deal goes through—I'm just a couple of weeks away. Tell her I'll pay her twenty percent interest." I knew the Santa Barbara deal was a real long shot, and here I hadn't even talked to Mom for weeks after that last phone call, and now I have to go crawling to her for help. But I didn't see that I had any choice— I couldn't lose the house, and I still believed that somehow he was going to pull us out of this.*
>
> *The evening at my mother's was one of the worst of my life. I pretended I was really enthusiastic about what Ben was working on—I repeated everything he told me to say. I showed her the architect's plans, the projected profits, and assured her we were almost there. I rationalized by telling myself that telling a little lie wasn't as bad as losing the house. She just shook her head and said, "I don't want to hear about that. Please don't insult my intelligence by repeating Ben's bull. I can understand why he sent you instead of coming over himself—he knows I'd tell him off. If you need to make your delinquent house payments, I'll give you the money. I don't want any interest—this is a gift, not a loan. You don't need any more debts hanging over your head. Now, you can get mad at me, but I have to say this. I'm very worried for you. I think Ben is reckless and irresponsible with money, and he's dragging you down with him. Now he's even got you lying for him."*

In the financial nightmare that Ben had created, his grandiose facade had crumbled. The man who told his wife in no uncertain terms that he would be in charge of their finances and that she didn't know anything about business was now looking to her to bail him out. And by continuing to lie for him, Diane was eating away at not only her good name but her self-respect.

BREAKING ALL THE RULES

Kathy, too, went against many of her principles and values when she let David talk her into calling in sick for him when he was too hungover to go to work:

God, I know all about enabling and how you have to let the other person face the consequences of his behavior, but it feels so different in theory than when it really happens to you. I figured I had two choices: make the call or let David get fired. It sounds easy in the abstract. But I knew if I didn't do this for him, he'd lose his job and get more withdrawn and depressed and probably sit around the house all day. I broke all the rules. I didn't call my sponsor, I didn't go to a meeting, I lied for him. He swore it would be the last time, but of course it wasn't.

Lying for an alcoholic was familiar territory for Kathy. She'd done the same thing for her mother. When she was only ten she would be told to call her mother's boss when her mother had been drinking heavily and tell him that her mother had the flu and wouldn't be coming in for a few days. Lying for someone you love became "what you do." And just as young Kathy believed she was doing the loving and loyal thing for her mother, so grown-up Kathy believed that she was doing the most loving thing for her husband.

The healthy part of Kathy knew that what she was doing was destructive not only for herself but for David as well. But when David worked on her sympathies, he reactivated her childhood feelings and experiences, and she fell back on old patterns of caretaking and covering up.

RAGE AND REVENGE

"I'll show him!"
"Who the hell does he think he is!"
"How dare he play me for a fool!"
"If he can do it so can I!"
"I never want to see him again as long as I live!"

Your lover's deception and betrayal may enrage you more than anything else in your life ever has. When the truth kicks you in the stomach, the drugs of denial and rationalization suddenly stop working and pain howls through you. In that moment, feelings and impulses outrun reason, and too often, so do your actions.

Allison had stubbornly refused to believe that Scott could ever cheat on her until she saw him in the front seat of his car locked in a passionate embrace with his assistant:

I saw his car parked near his office in Beverly Hills, and I slowed down to see if he might be taking a walk after lunch. Then I realized he was still in the car—with her. I've never been so hurt, so stunned or furious in my life. I'm amazed I didn't ram his car. I don't know how I got home—it's a blur. The tears were running down my face. I threw myself on the bed crying and screaming and beating the mattress. I knew I had to get back at that bastard. I wasn't going to be some pathetic victim. I was shaking with anger—I felt like I might explode into a million pieces. I've never felt like that before.

Understandably, Allison was running on pure rage, but the intensity of that rage shocked her. She'd pushed down her frustrations and suspicions for so long that when she couldn't stuff them any longer, they exploded. She felt disconnected from herself and frightened that she might totally lose control. As she kept rerunning the picture of Scott and the other woman embracing, she felt helpless and victimized—and she didn't like that picture of herself. She mistakenly decided that the best way to regain control was to retaliate against the person who had betrayed her.

I knew I'd feel better if I just did something. I took his prize stamp collection and poured stale coffee over it. Then I put his clothes in trash bags. His pictures, his CDs, his stuff from the medicine cabinet—I wanted every bit of him out of my life. Then I left and went to a movie. I relished the idea of him coming home to this disaster.

Allison was like a cyclone, trying to hurt Scott as much as he'd hurt her. The fantasy of grinding him into the ground was really getting her adrenaline pumping and providing a brief respite from her pain. Through vengeful actions Allison was creating an illusion of empowerment for herself.

What's Good for the Goose

If the betrayal is a sexual one, as it was in Allison's case, some women impulsively throw themselves into what is known in the vernacular as a revenge fuck. If he can do it to me, I can do it to him, they decide.

After venting her rage on Scott's belongings, Allison decided he hadn't been punished enough:

I was all set to call up one of our bachelor friends who I know is attracted to me. I was going to get drunk and go to bed with him and make sure Scott found out about it—that would really get to him. An eye for an eye, right? But some little spark of sanity made its way through all that craziness, and I realized that hurting him wouldn't cure how I was feeling. I have a friend who actually did what I was planning, and she felt much worse afterward.

Of course Allison's friend felt worse afterward. Revenge doesn't nourish or comfort you. Revenge keeps you preoccupied with the responses of your lover—*his* pain, *his* comeuppance, the lessons you'll teach *him*. Together, Allison and I came up with a different focus—a healing focus on *her*.

The Close Link between Rage and Grief

Even though Ben's lies were not about other women, Diane was no less distraught when she got a series of bounced check notices from the bank. It seems that Ben used the mortgage money they had gotten from Diane's mother to renew his option on his highly speculative Santa Barbara project:

How could I have been so blind? I put the money from my mother into our joint account and mailed a check for the back

*payments the following day. But he'd gotten to the bank before
my check had a chance to clear and withdrawn the money. Now
I'm not even sure the S&L will give us time to sell the house. I
put a lot into that house, Susan. I'm smart and I've had a lot of
success, but he must think I'm an idiot. One minute I'm furious
with him and the next I'm furious at myself. I'm crying all the
time, and I wonder if I'm going to make it. How could he do this
to us? What do I do with this anger? How do I get back at him?*

Cheating is not the only betrayal that will make you feel as if
your life is falling apart. Deception of any sort is an insult to your
intelligence and your dignity. Diane clearly articulated the close
connection between rage and grief as she whipsawed back and
forth between the two. In addition to her fury at Ben and her self-
reproach for having permitted things to go this far, she was also
deeply hurt and frightened. She was crying not only for the possible loss of her home but for all the other losses—trust, stability,
respect, and certainly love—that lying creates.

But like Allison, Diane was ultimately able to put her focus on
the changes which she could make that turned her life around.

THROW OUT THE BATHWATER, BUT YOU MAY
WANT TO SAVE THE BABY

It's human nature to lash out when we've been hurt, and I'm not
suggesting that you not get angry. But if you allow your rageful
impulses to take over when your wounds are fresh, you may say
or do things that cause irreparable harm.

Of course you're furious. You'd have to be a robot not to be.
But the impulse to file for divorce immediately, jump into bed
with someone else, burn his clothes, or change the locks so he
can't get in may backfire badly if you act it out.

Rage and revenge are really just the other side of the denial and
rationalization coin. They feel empowering because they're active
instead of passive. You think you're initiating things instead of just
reacting to what he's doing, but in reality, neither stance is in your
best interests and neither has a chance to set the stage for healthy,
self-respecting behavior that can change your life for the better.
Instead, rage and revenge feed each other in a continuous loop.

Even in situations like Allison's, which are direct wounds to your heart and soul, it's important to let the dust settle and give yourself time to fully evaluate your relationship before making any sort of major life decision. There may be something worthwhile to save.

DEGRADED BY JEALOUSY

Allison had been too complacent about Scott. Long after she was presented with information that there could be a problem, she continued with her denial that he could ever betray her. But once she found out that there was indeed another woman, she swung to the other extreme:

Things calmed down and we're doing all right. But I have to tell you I'm doing a lot of obsessing about "What if it happens again?" I don't think I could survive another experience like that. I'm suspicious all the time. If he smiles at a woman I get furious. I'm turning into some kind of harpy—everything I've always hated. When he's on the phone, I go into the bedroom and pick up the extension. I check his shirts, go through all his pockets. . . . I really hit bottom the other day. I was going through the trash cans looking for god knows what—a motel receipt, anything—and I stuck my hand into a bag of greasy chicken bones. I never felt so humiliated in my life. The next thing you know I'll be stalking him.

In her desperation to make sure she would not be tricked again, Allison became a detective, believing somehow that she could prevent another calamity by becoming excessively suspicious. But just as rage and revenge are the ineffective opposites of denial and rationalization, so is paranoia the ineffective opposite of complacency. If he's going to cheat on you, he will find a way to do it no matter how many times you go through his wallet. Your overzealousness won't prevent him from doing it again, and becoming a snoop will only make you feel demeaned and ashamed.

HOW HIS LIES AFFECT YOUR CHILDREN

If you have children, living with a liar has a profound effect on their lives as well as yours. If you show by your behavior that you place a low premium on honesty, your children will absorb that information. What you say is not nearly as important as what you do. You can tell your children always to be truthful and that people shouldn't lie, but when they see you making excuses, rationalizing, and covering up for a man who lies, they learn where you really stand. Let me show you what I mean.

In Chapter 1 you met a young woman named Paula whose husband, John, had promised not to do anything that was sexually uncomfortable for her but then became coercive about oral sex once they were married. John also made another promise before they got married that he broke in an extremely cruel way:

> One of the things that reassured me that this was the right man for me was the way he was so understanding and supportive about my having been raped. He said he would always be there for me, that I could tell him anything, that I could trust him with anything. He said he would cut off his arm before he would ever use that experience against me in any way. He knows I'm seeing you and trying to get help, but lately he's been bringing up my past. He says things like "I didn't know I was marrying somebody so damaged. You're really damaged merchandise." I begged him to be patient with me. Oh god, Susan, why can't I do this one thing for him?

I told Paula that a much better question would be, Why is John being so mean and rotten? Sex was not the issue here. John's behavior was. How dare he use Paula's traumatic and terrible experience as a club to try to get his way after he had promised never to do such a thing? And why did Paula allow John to lie to her, insult her, and then come to the conclusion that it was because there was something horribly wrong with her?

Paula had watched her mother put up with lies and abuse for years. She had seen her mother slide into the victim role and be too paralyzed by religious and family constraints to do anything about it. You see, Paula's parents are Carol and Ken; I was seeing two generations of women who married liars.

Carol had never said to Paula, "It's OK if your husband lies to you—just put up with it." She didn't have to. Her behavior delivered the message loud and clear.

This was Carol's legacy to her daughter—a daughter she truly loved and had tried to protect. But with the best intentions in the world, Carol had been a model of unhealthy, self-defeating passivity and acceptance, which had become ingrained in her daughter. Fortunately, the cycle was finally broken, as you will see in the second half of this book.

TEACHING THE WRONG LESSONS

As your children grow and your partner's lying continues to color your world, your children may be pulled into his lying in ways you never imagined. Do you remember how Laurie, the sculptor who was involved with the sociopathic counselor, told me that she had developed a high tolerance for Michael's lying? I asked her if she had any idea how she became so accepting of such unacceptable behavior:

Well, my father, whom I adored, was a chronic liar. He's a compulsive gambler, so of course there were constant lies about money. He's a car salesman and he made pretty decent money, but he spent it all at the track. We were rich one day and destitute the next. He was always making wild promises about things he was going to do for my brother and me—private schools, new cars. None of it ever happened, of course, but he was so charming and so much fun to be around that I could forgive him for constantly disappointing me. My mother was always angry with him, and as a kid I actually felt sorry for him, being married to such a shrew. There was a lot I didn't know.

Laurie soon discovered that money wasn't the only thing her charismatic father lied about, and it was a discovery that shattered her adolescent world:

I had cut some classes and sneaked off with my boyfriend to the McDonald's across from my high school. I was a little nervous someone might see us, so we sat in a back corner just flirting and having a good time. As we were leaving to go back to school, I saw this middle-aged couple nuzzling and kissing in a booth across the room. The woman was a redhead with too much makeup and a tight sweater. The man looked really familiar. Then I realized it was my father! He looked up and caught my eye. He kind of smiled and then turned away from me. My heart was beating so fast I thought it would jump out of my chest. I felt dizzy and totally disoriented. I mean, that was my father, and he's got a girlfriend!

My father never said a word about seeing me, and I never told anyone about seeing him. I felt like I had this terrible dirty secret. I certainly wasn't going to tell my mother, because she was always upset with him anyway and I didn't want to be the cause of more trouble between them. But at the same time I felt like I was betraying her. I felt so guilty!

By seeing something she shouldn't have seen and being drawn into silent complicity with her father, Laurie was forced to betray her mother—a terrible burden for any youngster to carry.

Laurie's father didn't speak to her directly about what happened, but she knew that she'd better keep his secret or risk losing his affection. Other fathers may overtly enlist their children's complicity to keep secrets, drawing them into a drama they should not be a part of. Some of my clients who grew up in households where there were major secrets and lies have reported that their fathers would actually confide in them about affairs they were having. As girls, they were told things like:

- "Don't tell your mother—it would kill her."
- "Don't tell your mother—it would destroy the family."
- "Don't tell your mother because she might leave me, and you might never be able to see me again."

What youngster wouldn't feel torn apart by the divided loyalties such demands for secrecy impose? In many ways, the dynamics are similar to incest. Your child is thrust into a role she is not mentally or emotionally capable of understanding. She is made to feel responsible for keeping the family together by keeping silent. And if she doesn't, she is sure that catastrophe will follow and it will be her fault if the family falls apart.

Children feel tremendous confusion when they are made the guardians of their fathers' lies. Laurie's father may not have felt any guilt or responsibility for his behavior, but Laurie certainly did when she was involved in his deception. Laurie grew up believing that she had no right to confront a man who lies and that the way you survive in a situation like that is to look the other way. I told Laurie that if she was ever going to overcome these unhealthy patterns, she'd better plan on developing a high intolerance for lying.

You are your children's first and most important teacher about relationships. If you continue to accept your partner's lies in order to maintain the facade of a stable family, you may very well set in motion the psychological mechanisms that perpetuate a high tolerance for lying in the next generation.

THE LOSS OF THE REAL YOU

Lying hurts everyone. It hurts the people you care about, but most of all it hurts you. Your emotional, mental, and physical health suffer. You find yourself developing characteristics that are totally alien to you. You may become hardened, hopeless, filled with negativity. You live with stress and tension that erode every facet of your well-being. You may believe, as Carol did, that going along is your best option, but look at what it cost her:

I had to convince myself things would work out. I'm Mormon and there's never been a divorce in our family. But I was becoming a different woman from the one I was when we got married. I lost a lot of my spirit, my faith in people, my confidence—the best parts of myself.

Carol is describing the keen sense of loss and emptiness that inevitably follows when you give up parts of yourself in order to keep a relationship. When your lover's deceptive behavior goes unchallenged and unchecked, a major metamorphosis in personality and emotional health takes place. Your moods go on a downward spiral. As self-respect fades, depression and hopelessness may become constant companions.

NOTHING STAYS THE SAME

You might believe, as Carol did, that you can get by with accepting things the way they are—and for a while you might. I know that every woman who is with a lover who lies cherishes the fantasy that one day he will confess everything, apologize for the hurt he's caused, beg for forgiveness, and immediately run to therapy.

But lying, like any unhealthy behavior, doesn't magically disappear, and it usually gets worse over time. Your partner will become more entrenched in his behavior and less willing to change. And you will find yourself giving up more and more of your self-respect and dignity.

But the real you hasn't vanished. Together we will find you again, and begin to heal the wounds that deception and betrayal have inflicted. At the same time, you will learn the only behaviors that can dramatically alter the painful patterns of your relationship and your life. It's time to put an end to the lying.

PART TWO

Healing the Wounds of Betrayal and Deception

In this section of the book, I'm going to teach you a powerful set of skills for dealing with your lover's lies, whether you've just discovered the first lie or whether the lying has been going on for years. I'll show you how to move into a clear, rational space from which you can make decisions that are in your best interests. I'll show you exactly what to say when you catch your lover in a lie, and I'll give you precise scripts for responding to his broad repertoire of appeals, explanations, and criticisms. You'll learn how to say, through both words and behavior, "The lying must stop!"

At the same time, I'll show you the most effective techniques I know for relieving your inner turmoil. I'll guide you through the process of dealing with your fear and anger using writing, visualizations, and rituals; then I'll help you grieve the loss of trust and bind up your wounds.

As you've seen, denial doesn't work, rationalizing doesn't work, and going ballistic, though it may give a momentary feeling of being in control, doesn't work either. What does work is combining your emotional work with behavioral strategies that allow you to confront the lying, decide what you will and won't accept, and, when possible, lay the foundation for a much more honest relationship.

In the case of the most destructive lies, I will help you carefully

evaluate whether it's healthier for you to stay in or end a relationship with the man who's been lying to you. If you stay, I'll help you
move toward putting an end to the lying and building a new relationship based on candor and respect. If after exploring all your
options, you decide that you cannot maintain your emotional well-
being if you stay, I'll help you through that difficult time.

As you do this work, please promise yourself that you will do
more than just read. Make a commitment to take the exercises off
the page and put them into your life each time you have an opportunity. Some of the communication techniques and the ways you'll
be learning to manage your emotions may seem totally foreign to
you at first. But I know from my own personal experience, as well
as my work with hundreds of women in situations very much like
yours, that they get easier and more comfortable with practice. And
they work! As an added bonus, they will also work with anyone else
in your life who lies to you.

While you can learn these behavioral strategies immediately
and on your own, I know there are times when the anxiety,
depression, and panic of discovering that your lover is a liar can
be so frightening and overwhelming that it's only common sense
to get some outside support. None of this work is intended to
replace therapy or support groups, but rather to provide an
important companion to whatever other personal growth work
you choose to do.

As you let new words, new thoughts, and new actions take
root, you'll see your life begin to change for the better. It won't
always be easy, but I promise you that each change you make will
have large reverberations in your life and take you closer to the
kind of relationship you want and deserve.

Remember, when it comes to making your life better, action
is your friend, and passivity is your enemy. So let's get to it!

7

The Moment of Truth

From the moment you decide you must deal with your lover's lying, you may experience some of the most intense heartbreak, uncertainty, anger, and fear you've ever encountered. Whether the lies are new or familiar, it may seem overwhelming to have to make decisions or to take any kind of action. The relationship—and the world you knew—has changed forever.

- If you've just discovered the lying, you probably feel so hurt, so wounded, that you believe the only thing you have the strength to do is let the storm of emotions carry you until it loses its force. I know you feel panicked and uncertain of what to do next.
- If you've been dealing with a history of lying and have been hiding your feelings, you may find that your anger has turned to depression and bitterness. You may have temporarily regained your footing, but you're living with a sense of waiting for the next shoe to drop—for the next lie, the next terrible shock to your system. You may also be expending a lot of emotional energy ignoring the anger you feel when you allow yourself to think about his betrayal.
- If you've left a relationship with a liar, you may feel vulnerable and unsure of how to keep from being deceived again. You don't know how to find the middle ground between suspicion and complacency. The old pain and

anger may seem dulled most of the time but may flare up with startling power, even when you think you've moved on. You may be determined that things will be different the next time but still not be sure how to protect yourself. You are probably also dealing with a lot of painful self-reproach.

Whatever your personal scenario may be, and wherever you are in the process of dealing with a liar, I hope you will make a commitment to yourself to do the active, courageous work required to move past the hurt into a better life.

THE VERY FIRST STEP

Let's take first things first: you're in the midst of an emotional upheaval. This is not a good time to make any major life decisions. It is not a good time to listen to, or attempt to evaluate, your lover's explanations of what has happened, and it's certainly not a good time to try to determine whether your relationship can continue. The volume on your feelings is turned up so high right now that your emotions are distorting and limiting the way you process information—even if you feel calm and think you are being very rational. None of this applies to a relationship with a sociopath, where getting out is the only decision you need to make, and you must do that now.

If you are dealing with a long-standing situation, you need to look at the ways you've responded in the past, as well as what hasn't worked for you and how you can change your half of the interaction between you.

Resolve right now to put yourself in a holding pattern for the next seven days. This is your time to gain the clarity and strength you'll need to deal with this crisis. I know you're feeling a great sense of urgency, but let's direct that urgency toward your healing and away from what to do about him. We have a lot of work to do.

FIVE C's FOR DEALING WITH A LOVER'S LIES

If you're like most women, no one has taught you how to move through and beyond the pain, the havoc, and the chaos that a lover's lying creates. But the five steps—or five C's—that I'll guide you through in this and the following chapters will provide an extremely effective structure for facing what's happened to you with dignity and a true sense of empowerment. I'll list the steps here for you, so you'll have a map of where we're going. You might think of this list as vitamin C for the wounds of betrayal and deception.

1. CREATE an environment that allows you to focus on yourself.
2. CENTER: Find the still place inside yourself that enables you to think clearly.
3. CONFRONT: Tell your lover what you've discovered, how it has made you feel, and what you want from him now.
4. Set CONDITIONS: Once you have decided what you want, what you will and won't accept, and what your conditions are for continuing the relationship, express them to your lover.
5. CONNECT with supportive family members, friends, and, when indicated, mental-health professionals. In particular, I urge you to tap the healing power of women's friendship.

Once you have put the five C's into action, you will be far more able to decide what your next steps will be and whether or not you have a relationship that is worth salvaging.

CREATING THE RIGHT ENVIRONMENT

To help reduce some of the pressure on you, I strongly urge you to spend time away from your partner during this first week. You need to focus on yourself and not deal with him until you're less off balance. The first thing I want you to say to him is:

I need some time by myself to sort things out. I would appreciate it if you could stay somewhere else for a week, or at least a few days, until I feel ready to talk about what's happened.

Even if your realization that he's lied to you was several days or weeks ago, I still want you to make that statement. It immediately reverses the balance of power and makes you active instead of passive.

Your lover may not be at all happy with your request. It may scare him. It definitely means he's going to be inconvenienced and will have to alter his routine. He may do a full-court press to assure you that you can work this out together. If he follows you from room to room crying, pleading, or pressuring you to talk to him, hang tough and tell him you will talk to him when you're ready. Remember, what he wants comes second. He's been doing what he wants for a while now.

If the two of you aren't living together, it's a lot easier to create this environment. If you're married or living together and your partner isn't willing or able to stay somewhere else, maybe you can. It's difficult to start the healing process while the two of you are battling back and forth or he's working on your sympathies. If you have children, I know that makes the situation more complicated, but do try. It's critical to get some breathing space while you begin regrouping.

If it isn't feasible for either of you to stay somewhere else for a short period of time, then at least make sure to set aside as many private hours for yourself as you can.

Whether he is with you or not, you need to rearrange your schedule to include time for yourself. I know that isn't always easy, but consider these possibilities:

- Take a week, or at least a few days, off from work.
- If you can't take even a full day off, take an afternoon or a long lunch. Claim whatever time you can.

As you can see, the very first order of business is to clear the decks as much as possible so that you have the time and emotional environment you need. Sit down with a calendar right now and mark down the time—at least two hours a day—that you will devote to your well-being. During that time, no television, no phone calls.

WHAT TO SAY TO YOUR CHILDREN

I know it's hard to think about so many things when you're feeling overwhelmed, but if you have children, you are going to have to decide how to help them through this difficult time. If they are infants or toddlers, it would be best if they could stay with a grandparent, another relative, or a friend for at least the first few days of this week. Little ones, as you well know, require an enormous amount of physical and emotional energy, and right now you may barely have enough to get yourself through the day.

If your children are older and need to stay with you because of school or other valid reasons, you need to let them know something about why you are so upset. The amount of information you give your children at this time will, of course, depend on their age. But if they are over four or five, you must tell them something. Children are incredibly intuitive and perceptive. They absorb their parents' tensions like a sponge, and they are entitled to an explanation that will allow them to understand that you are upset and need some time to yourself.

Jan's children were ten and twelve when she discovered the truth about Bill's second ex-wife on their mortgage loan application. At first she thought she could keep her upset from the children:

> *Look, they don't need to know what's going on. They're so involved with their own friends and activities they probably won't even notice. This is between Bill and me, and I don't see any reason to involve them. He's still new to them, and I want them to have a good relationship with him.*

I told Jan that she didn't need to go into the details of what she'd discovered, but she was fooling herself if she thought she could pretend everything was peachy. Together we worked out some appropriate things for her to say to her children, and the following week she told me how grateful she was that I had urged her to do this:

> *At first I thought you were pushing me to do something that didn't feel right, but then I realized that if we're going to change*

things, I don't want to keep secrets and have to put on an act. It
takes too much out of me. So I told them that Bill and I were
having some problems that had absolutely nothing to do with
them. I told the kids I was upset and that I was angry with him,
but we were getting help to work things out. I said that they
would probably see me crying sometimes and that it was OK—
they didn't need to fix it for me—that was my job. The first
thing they wanted to know was whether Bill and I were getting
a divorce. I told them I didn't think so, but I couldn't promise
right now.

Then my older girl said something that touched me so
deeply. She said, "Thanks, Mom, for having this talk with us.
We knew something was wrong but we didn't know what. I sure
hope things work out, but the important thing is for you to be
happy." I think she's twelve going on forty.

Jan gave her children a great gift—the gift of truth. By validat-
ing their perceptions that there was indeed trouble between Bill
and herself, and assuring them it wasn't their fault (the first thing
children usually assume), she could relieve them from the confusing speculations that children indulge in when they're not told
at least a little of what's happening between their parents. She
also did something else that was quite wonderful. She let her children know that it was her responsibility, not theirs, to deal with
how she was feeling and to resolve the situation between their
step-father and herself. She didn't ask them to take sides or put
them in the middle.

If you try to pretend that nothing's wrong in the midst of your
emotional storm, you will confuse and bewilder your children
and take away their ability to trust not only their perceptions but
your truthfulness as well.

You can use the same basic format Jan did to communicate
your feelings to them. If your children are older, you can decide
how many details you want to share with them, especially if
they're adults. But even then, it's important not to pull them in
and look to them to resolve the crisis for you. That will only
make them feel overwhelmed and inadequate.

DEALING WITH OTHER PEOPLE

Another important part of creating a healing environment is deciding what to do about your relationships with other people in your life.

I strongly suggest that you keep your own counsel for this first week and have minimal contact with friends and family. Your thoughts and feelings have a lot to tell you, and it's a good idea not to be distracted by other people.

Realistically, I know you feel alone and isolated after what's happened to you, and you probably yearn to reach out to someone for comfort, but my concern is that other people, as well-meaning as they may be, are prone to bombard you with conflicting advice. If someone close to you calls or wants to see you, it's helpful to say something like:

I'm dealing with some very difficult events right now and I need a little time to get myself together. I'll talk to you very soon, but right now I need a few days to myself.

If that's not comfortable for you, and you really want to see or talk to someone, make sure you set some ground rules. You can say:

I appreciate your concern, but I need you just to listen/hold me/hear me out/let me cry. I don't expect you to fix it, and I really don't want any advice about what to do. That's my job to figure out, and that's what I'm doing.

Once you've structured your emotional environment, you're ready to begin the next phase.

FINDING A CALM CENTER

If you've ever seen photographs taken from the eye of a hurricane, you have a good image of the kind of shift you'll need to make in order to start dealing with what's happening to you.

Swirling around of the eye are the destructive winds that flatten everything in their path and fill up with debris. The center of the cloud, though, is a still, light space that moves like a spotlight across the land, illuminating the damage of the wind.

I know that words like *calm* and *centered* may seem incongruous to you in the context of the emotional storm that's inevitably stirred up by a lover's lying. It's perfectly normal and human to get caught in the circling, cycling feelings that surround the lies. You're filled with rage and panic—how in the world are you supposed to be calm? You may have had several explosions already, and yelled and screamed all kinds of invectives at him.

Don't worry—it was a perfectly human response. But you don't want to get stuck in the volatile realm of pure emotions. You want to be able to look clearly at what's happened and prepare for what you need to do next. You will still have your feelings and the valuable information they provide, but you will be able to think rationally as well.

Simplistic as it may sound, the first thing I want you to do is stop and take a couple of deep breaths. Now let yourself absorb three vitally important facts. The following statements are true for any situation where you have found that you've been lied to, and you may want to say them aloud several times when you need to calm yourself:

I am entitled to what I feel.
I will survive.
I don't have to make any decisions until I'm ready.

Words have enormous power, and the effects of self-talk can't be overestimated.

Let these three simple phrases become your mantra for this first week.

Also, let your partner know in no uncertain terms that you will not be pressured into a premature answer or decision because he's upset or demanding to know what you're planning to do. Don't defend or try to explain.

Tell him:

"I'm sorry you're upset, but I need some time to think."
"I knew you wouldn't be happy about this, but that's the way it has to be."

> "I know you're upset, but I'm going to take as much time
> as I need to decide what to do next."

I strongly urge you to engage in as much physical activity as
you can. You need to get those all-important endorphins going to
help you feel better. A lover's lies can immobilize you with depression, and it's tempting to take to your bed and pull the covers over
your head. That's the worst thing you can do. Get out and walk,
even if it's just for fifteen minutes. If you go to a gym, use the punch-
ing bag. As you use your body, repeat your calming phrases. Physical activity is rhythmic, and you can actually walk the words into
your feelings and your body as well as your mind.

ANGER: THE FRIGHTENING FEELING

A crucial part of your centering is dealing with your anger at your
lover. You can do that by first taking a look at your traditional
ways of dealing with anger. When a woman realizes she's been
lied to, she generally responds in two ways—by acting out or acting in. Acting out is an attempt to defend against emotional pain
by temporarily dulling it with some kind of behavior, usually
vengeful and self-defeating. Acting in means that we turn the pain
against ourselves. Most women tend to do one more than the
other, but many swing back and forth between the two until they
learn more effective ways of responding.

Acting Out

Let's deal with acting out first.
    If you tend to act out, your anger may prompt you to:

Destroy things that are important to him (e.g., his car, his
    family heirlooms)
Inform his wife of your affair with him, if he's married to
    someone else
Go to his place of business and make a scene
Call everyone you can think of and tell them what a bas-
    tard he is
Start divorce proceedings immediately

When Allison damaged Scott's stamp collection and bundled up his clothes in trash bags after discovering his affair, she was turning her pain into dramatic, colorful actions that gave her a momentary sense of being in control and took her mind off her misery:

I can't deny I got a kind of maniacal glee out of what I did. But now I feel guilty and ashamed. The worst of it is, I still want to hurt him the way he hurt me. Nothing's changed—I still feel awful.

Acting out can leave you with an emotional hangover, a sense of remorse that only magnifies how bad you feel. As I showed Allison, it's possible to release anger without escalating it, or compounding it with feelings of despair.

Allison had a lot to say to Scott, so I asked her to use an empty chair to symbolize her husband and encouraged her to let him know in no uncertain terms how furious she was. There was a stream of I-hate-you-I-hate-yous followed by lots of tears.

Allison: I hate him right now, but I haven't given up hope totally. . . .

Susan: Right now the main question on your mind is "How can I hurt him the most?" Is there another question you can think of that would put the focus back on you?

Allison: Yeah—"How could he do this to me?" I mean, the thing is, I've got these layers of rage. I can't pretend I don't. And I just don't know how to turn off that loud voice that says, "Don't take it. Get back at him."

Susan: How about asking "What's the most effective thing I can do for myself right now?" What does that feel like?

Allison: I'm not sure—he hasn't been punished enough—

Susan: Say it aloud a few times: "What's the most effective thing I can do for myself right now?"

Allison did just that, and acknowledged that shifting her focus from revenge against Scott to her own well-being was calming and gave her a glimmer of hope in what had been a very dark few days. The empty chair is always available if you want to vent your emotions, but remember to keep asking that all-important question: What can I do for myself right now? Jot down the answers that come to mind—they'll help you slow down long enough to tap your inner wisdom, and they'll provide real guidance if you stay focused on yourself.

Acting In

Allison had little trouble contacting her anger, but many women are terrified of this emotion. When I looked up the words *rage* and *anger* in the dictionary, I was startled to see how much of the definitions of both words, while including phrases like "strong emotions" and "a reaction to being injured," also referred to losing control and, even worse, madness. No wonder so many women deny and repress their anger—who wants to be seen as a raving lunatic?

I've often seen how frightening it is for many women to deal with their anger, especially toward their lovers. Through the years I have heard statements like:

"I'll go crazy."
"I'll hurt someone."
"I'll split into a million pieces."
"I'll look hideous."
"Nobody likes an angry woman."

But the anger has to go somewhere—it doesn't just stay stuffed forever. When it doesn't go out to the external world, it gets stored in our internal world. And oh, what damage it can do!

Women who *don't* act out turn their feelings against themselves. They may:

Think obsessively about the lying, as if by replaying events in their heads, they will find some clue or answer—especially about what they did to cause the betrayal
Have trouble eating and sleeping
Become depressed or highly anxious

Develop physical complaints
Drink or eat too much
Have trouble concentrating or functioning
Become irritable
Cry all the time

I'm sure you get the idea. Downplaying your pain and anger may help you avoid confrontation or unpleasant encounters with your lover, but the price is much too high.

Diane's husband, Ben, had just about wiped them out financially through his series of bad business gambles, and the couple saw that they would probably have to file for bankruptcy. Diane was tremendously upset, but she kept her anger tightly reined in:

I've been wearing sunglasses all the time because my eyes are so red and swollen. I need to talk about this, but I don't know what to say, especially to my mother. I don't think I can stand the knowing looks and the I-told-you-so's. I guess it's better to suffer in silence . . . but I'm so tired all the time. I'm tossing and turning all night worrying. I feel like the biggest idiot in the world—how could I let him do this to me?

Diane was struggling with depression and self-reproach and had no clue about how to cope. But she wasn't just suffering in silence—she had come into therapy because she knew she needed direction. Where Allison was learning to manage the cauldron of rage she knew she was carrying around, Diane needed to contact and externalize the anger she was turning against herself.

I set up a role-playing situation in which I would play Ben. I encouraged Diane to start ten sentences with "How dare you" and to fill in the rest. I know from experience that for women who are afraid of their anger, those three words serve as a powerful catalyst that quickly and effectively helps them connect with their angry feelings.

I reassured Diane that she was safe and that under no circumstances would I push her too far. I told her she was in complete control and could stop whenever she wanted to. The same is true for you. If you do this work on your own, you can use the empty chair as I did with Allison, or write a how-dare-you letter, which you may or may not ultimately read or give to your partner. Whether you do this anger work with someone you trust or by yourself, I want to give you the same assurance I gave Diane. You are in charge, and you only go as far as is comfortable for you.

Diane started hesitantly, as I expected, and her how-dare-you's were quite timid at first, but I could see and hear them becoming more angry as we went on.

Diane (to me as Ben): How dare you lie to me about your crazy deals! How dare you take money out of the bank without telling me? How dare you make me lie to my mother?

At the mention of her mother, Diane began to tear up. I told her no tears for right now—those were easy for her. I wanted her to stay with her anger—which she most certainly did.

Diane: You've ruined our lives—you son of a bitch!
Susan (as Ben): Honey—you don't know how sorry I am. I did what I thought was best for us—please forgive me. I swear I'll get us out of this. I just need a little time.
Diane: Susan, have you been hiding in my house? That's just what he's been saying!
Susan: Which makes you feel–
Diane: Which makes me feel furious and tricked and like a fool.

Once Diane's anger was put into words and externalized, it lost a lot of the fearsome power it had over her:

I was always taught that nice girls don't get angry. I've always tried to reason everything out . . . be the peacemaker, be the logical, controlled one. It was really tough for me to show so much anger, even to you . . . but it wasn't as scary as I thought it was going to be.

It rarely is. If you tend to turn your anger against yourself, it is because your apprehension about what might happen if you allowed yourself to experience those feelings is more terrible, in your mind, than the suffering that acting in inevitably causes. But in reality, the consequences of getting angry are rarely as catastrophic as you think they'll be. And the only way you can know that is to have the courage to do what Diane did—contact and express your scariest feelings.

As she worked with her anger, Diane began to feel her energy returning. It had taken tremendous strength to keep from expressing her feelings, and as she learned to face them instead of holding them in, that strength became available for the work of rebuilding her life.

There is no one magic way to deal with the pain and rage of betrayal. You need to find what works best for you. You may have already expressed some or even a lot of your feelings to your partner—and that's OK. In the next chapter I'll show you the most effective things to say to him. In the meantime, writing a how-dare-you letter, or verbalizing your anger to an empty chair or a picture of your lover, works wonderfully for some women. There are anger workshops you can go to. You can whack a tennis ball or pound your pillow. You can express your anger through writing or drawing. The bottom line is, try these things and find what works for you. The more you can express your anger in a structured way, the less you'll feel driven to act out or turn your anger against yourself.

A vital part of the centering process involves calming the impulse to flail about creating as much havoc as possible and the impulse to beat up on yourself, letting your body express your distress through a variety of physical and emotional pains. You cannot feel whole if parts of your emotional life are either over-controlled or exiled to some deep recess of your inner world.

Give yourself an assignment to do some of this important emotional work today.

ACKNOWLEDGING YOUR LOSSES

As you continue the centering process, you'll find that there is a complex and shifting constellation of emotions that either runs parallel to anger or quickly follows it. The most prominent of these is grief.

Your grief can be a pulse of sadness, sometimes booming, sometimes almost imperceptible, but always a backdrop to discovering betrayal. Anger and rage, as you've seen, not only don't preclude grief—they're actually woven into it. Even if you've been able to contact and express your anger, you've probably been doing a lot of crying too.

That's because there has been a death, not of an actual person but of the relationship you had, which can never be the same again. And along with it, many of your hopes and beliefs, your sense of trust, and your emotional security have died. A serious lie is a wound to the heart. If you have been living with lies for some time, you've probably experienced a loss of confidence and self-respect as well. These multiple deaths must be grieved in order to heal from them.

As with anger, people's responses to grief are many and varied. The one thing I can tell you is that grief cannot be sidestepped. You need to go through it, not around it or over it or under it as many people try to do. Grief hurts like hell, and I don't blame anyone for trying to avoid it, but the problem is, it can't be skipped—it can only be delayed. And the longer you delay facing it, the harder it gets.

WRITING A GRIEF LETTER

One of the most effective exercises I know to help you start to deal with your grief and diminish it over the next several weeks is to write a grief letter. I know how important it is to have a container for your feelings when they seem fragmented and overwhelming. This letter allows you to explore what you have lost and to express your feelings about those losses in a safe, focused way. To help you structure your own letter, I'm going to share Anne's with you. I think it's an excellent guide.

> *To my grief:*
> *Well—you found me, didn't you. I didn't want you in my life, but here you are—at least for a while. What's the matter—did you think I had it too good? Well, as*

*long as you're here I might as well deal with you so I
can get rid of you, because you are definitely an unwel-
come visitor.*

*As you know, I found out that Randy betrayed my
trust and our marriage vows. I know that happens to
lots of people, but knowing that doesn't help one damn
bit when it happens to you. And I'm not willing to say,
"Oh, that's just the way men are." I hurt.*

So here's my grief list:

> *I'm grieving the loss of what I thought I could
>   always be sure of—that I had a husband I could
>   trust and who loved me and would be faithful to
>   me.*
> *I'm grieving the loss of my confidence in my
>   desirability and attractiveness.*
> *I'm grieving the loss of a very special man who is
>   not who I thought he was. I miss him, and I can
>   never get him back.*
> *I'm grieving the loss of the clean, safe love I
>   thought I had. That's tarnished now.*
> *I'm grieving the loss of a certain kind of innocence.
>   Not a child's innocence, but an innocence about
>   "it can't happen to me." It can and it did.*
> *I'm grieving the loss of the relationship I had, but
>   holding onto the hope that a new one will take
>   its place. I will work very hard to help that
>   happen.*

*But I want you to know, grief, that I'm putting you on
notice. I know you're going to hang around for a while,
but your days are definitely numbered. You will not
destroy me.*

*Yours truly
(you didn't expect me
to say love, did you?),
Anne*

Many elements of Anne's letter will work well for you. There is an acceptance of things as they are and a recognition that her marriage must be rebuilt. Anne also took a firm stand with her grief and expressed her determination to get through it. Although there is great sadness in her letter, there's also some humor and spunkiness. This is not a victim's letter—it's the letter of a fighter.

At this moment, you may believe that there's no way you can be that strong. Well, I can assure that you Anne didn't feel as clear and determined as she sounded. But she laid out some important emotional goals for herself with her letter—goals she would ultimately reach.

In the middle of grieving, it's natural to believe that you will hurt forever, but you won't. While the pain is still intense, be very kind to yourself. Cry all you want, but make time for nourishing, healing activities too. Above all, remember: you are stronger than you feel. I know it's tough, but do your best not to obsess twenty-four hours a day about what's happened. Grief really does come to an end. You will find the spirit and the strength that are the center of your being. You will survive.

THAT AWFUL FEAR

At this time, a strong undertow may seem to pull you into a dark, churning place. This force is not anger or grief but fear. As in a bad dream, the hallways of fear are lined with mirrors, each reflecting a different face:

- Fear of change
- Fear of the unknown
- Fear of being alone
- Fear of having to start over again
- Fear that you won't make it
- Fear that you'll never be able to trust again

Perhaps, you think, the fear would be manageable if it had a clear outline, if you could just see it. But it feels fluid. Its shape-shifting leaves you feeling paralyzed at the time when you most need to function effectively. And it can take on enormous proportions.

When she recognized that her marriage to David might not survive, Kathy began experiencing symptoms that were totally new to her:

My mind jumps from one thing to another, my heart's pounding, I'm nauseous half the time, and everywhere I look, all I can see is heartache and loneliness. I still have to work, but god, it's hard. I'm crying all the way to work and all the way home. I can handle almost anything, but this has thrown me for a loop. What's happening to me?

I told Kathy that what she was experiencing was not just fear, but fear in its most intense form: panic. This was her reaction:

You know, it helps just to have a name for it. It's not like a full-blown panic disorder, like some people have where they can't leave the house, but it's more than fear. I mean, I'm afraid of snakes and spiders, but this is different. It's more like when I was little and afraid of the dark. I was sure there was something terrible out there and I didn't know what. My mom would come in and turn on the light and sit with me, and after a few minutes I'd be OK. But I feel like there's no light to turn on now—like I've just got this thing that's sitting on my chest and holding me down.

If these feelings and images describe a lot of what you're experiencing, you, like Kathy, need to find some ways to turn on the light—but as an adult, not a child.

For the purposes of your work here, it's important that you not go back into childhood now. In crisis, you need all of your adult coping mechanisms to see you through, and they can be weakened by the inevitable regression that occurs when you dredge up the old feelings of helplessness and dependency that are normal for children. You can work on unfinished business from your childhood later if you choose, but right now you need to connect with your adult strengths.

I have found that when fear becomes an amorphous cloud that threatens to envelop you, it's extremely effective to give it a face—literally. Follow the work I did with Kathy and try the same exercise yourself.

I handed Kathy a copy of *National Geographic* magazine and asked her to look through it until she found a picture of something that reminded her of the "thing" that was sitting on her chest. A magazine like *National Geographic*, which shows a variety of subjects—animals as well as unusual people and places—works particularly well for this exercise. Kathy found a story on coal mines and was immediately struck by the pictures. Now we had a specific image to work with, a point of focus in the darkness, so it wouldn't feel so vast and undifferentiated. I put the picture on a chair and told Kathy to get the black pit off her chest. I asked her to close her eyes. Then I turned off the lights in the office and asked Kathy to speak to her panic:

"I can't breathe—I have to get out . . ."

I stopped her and spoke quietly to keep from interrupting her visualization:

"Kathy, try saying 'I will get out of here' instead of 'I have to.' Start again and see if that doesn't feel less panicky."

"I can't breathe with you here. I know you're trying to bury me inside you, but I will get out." She smiled and said, "Yeah, that feels a lot better." Then she really began to sound stronger. "I don't want you, I don't need you—get the hell out of my life! I will come up to the surface. I will turn on the light."

I wasn't surprised at the shift in Kathy's demeanor. She relaxed noticeably. Even though I've been doing this work for a quarter of a century, it never fails to amaze me that a small change in the way we say something can have such a dramatic impact on our determination and perceptions. By simply substituting a firm "I will" for the more panicky sounding "I have to," Kathy began the process of calming herself and facing her panic head-on.

"Good, Kathy," I said. "Now I want you to visualize climbing out of the pit. I know it's dark and scary, but you only need to see the path immediately in front of you—not the whole picture. You're an expert at taking one day at a time. For right now, you only need to take one moment at a time. Now go and turn on the light."

I pointed out to her that you can use a light switch or a candle to symbolize being able to choose between spinning in the darkness or illuminating your path. This simple action is one that I would like you to do several times a day. Experience the darkness and how it feeds and powers your panic, making you feel like a lost child. Then choose to turn on the light, both literally and figuratively. It will help you find your way.

It's also a good idea to tape-record some of the reassuring, calming statements I made to Kathy and play them back to yourself while you're doing this exercise. If that doesn't feel comfortable for you, ask someone with whom you feel close and safe to do it for you.

The intensity of your fears, like your anger and grief, will diminish. But in the meantime, life has to go on. You need to function. The world doesn't stop making demands on you because you've discovered your lover is a liar. Certainly the work in this book will help you regain your bearings. So will working with a mental-health professional or joining some kind of support group. You need to take advantage of every resource at your disposal. If your depression and anxiety become unmanageable, I urge you to consider speaking to a physician. Some new medications have proven enormously effective in alleviating extremes of the mood spectrum. I'm not suggesting that a pill will solve all your problems, only that some of the drugs developed in recent years are valuable tools for getting you back on your feet and speeding the process of recovering your emotional balance.

I realize that I've thrown a lot of information and work at you at a time when you're already feeling overwhelmed. You don't need to do every exercise, but I urge you to do the ones that speak the most personally to you. Working with these exercises will not magically "fix" you or completely take away your painful feelings. You've been wounded, and healing from your wounds is a process that we're just beginning.

But this work will prepare you to move toward firm, self-caring behavior. By calming and comforting yourself, you are showing yourself true kindness, respect, and love.

8

Confrontation and Clarity

My hope is that you're feeling calmer now. I know there's a great temptation to want to stay in a holding pattern, but the purpose of the calming work you did in the last chapter was not to anesthetize yourself, so that you could resume old patterns with your lover, but to help you mobilize to take the next step: confrontation.

If the sound of that word made you tense, you're not alone. Confrontation is one of the scariest words in the language because most people don't understand what it's really about and tend to equate it with physical battling, screaming matches, or power plays. You may believe that confronting someone means trying to overpower them and win at all costs. But confrontation is not about combat. It's about clarity.

You badly need clarity about how much your relationship has been damaged and whether there's a future for it, and the structured confrontation I will guide you through will provide it. You'll learn to speak up about what you want, and to listen and ask questions until you understand what your lover is willing to do. Don't worry that you will have to master this powerful new skill alone. I'll tell you exactly what to say, when and how to say it, how to respond to his responses, and how to get the information you need to decide what to do next. We'll get there step by step.

IT'S NORMAL TO FEEL ANXIOUS

Before we get to the nuts and bolts of confrontation, let me answer some of the questions and concerns you probably have about it.

Jan was concerned about how she was going to look to Bill:

You know, I'm really confident at work, and I have a lot of authority there. I'm not afraid to tell people what I want. But this . . . I don't know that he's ever seen that side of me. I don't want to come off like a total bitch. I feel like I'll have to turn into a different person to do something like this.

Helen, whose husband, Phil, had become heavily involved in on-line sex, had another kind of concern:

I've already confronted him. I've told him how sneaky and sleazy I think he is and that this has got to stop. I don't know that there's any more I can say—I've read him the riot act already—the ball's in his court now.

Anne, whose husband, Randy, had the brief affair with a woman at work, was totally focused on how he might react rather than on what she needed to do for herself:

I'm scared he'll get really upset. We seem to be doing OK. I know we're not really dealing with anything, but maybe things can just get better by themselves. He hates all this touchy-feely, expressing-your-feelings-all-the-time stuff.

Diane was afraid she would do it "wrong":

I know I'll screw this up. I'll probably break down if I try to talk to him about what he's done to us. Can't I just insist that I handle all financial matters from now on?

Pat, the antique shop owner you met in Chapter 2, worked very hard to convince me that she didn't have the "right" to confront her boyfriend, Paul, about his sleeping with an ex-girlfriend:

*Look, we're not married or engaged, so why should I make a
big production out of it? He's apologized, and I think he's really
sorry. He knows he screwed up. I don't want to look like a jealous, possessive shrew.*

But certainly one of the most unusual concerns came from
Ruth, whose successful lawyer husband, Craig, had been compul-
sively cheating on her with a number of women.

Ruth expressed a strong desire to "try to work things out." I
told her that I wasn't very optimistic about Craig's willingness or
even ability to make the changes necessary for them to have any
kind of future together. The only way there was even a ghost of a
chance was if she were to confront Craig and insist that he participate in some specific treatment (including regular attendance
in a program for sexual addicts). I could see "Yes, but . . ." written
all over her face.

When I asked her why she was so hesitant about my suggestions, she answered, "I believe in unconditional love. You're asking me to set a lot of conditions."

Amazing! Here's a woman whose husband has behaved atro-
ciously, who has lied untold numbers of times, and who appears
to have no moral compass whatever, and she's worried about
unconditional love!

All these concerns, and others like them that I've heard over
the years, are really elaborate forms of resistance to avoid confrontation. So let's put them to rest.

1. No, you won't look like a bitch or a shrew if you follow the
   scripts I'll give you. It is neither bitchy nor shrewish to
   become proactive in confronting your lover and deciding if
   the relationship is salvageable. It is healthy and self-
   respectful.
2. No, it's not enough that you yelled and screamed at him.
   That makes him defensive so that he's not able to hear or
   process anything you're saying to him. It does nothing to
   create an atmosphere in which anything can be resolved.
   What Helen did was assault and attack. That's not a
   confrontation.

3. Yes, he may get upset. So what? Can't you tolerate some discomfort in the service of your growth and possibly the salvation of the relationship? He's been upset before, and he'll undoubtedly be upset again, and neither of you will die from it.

4. No, I don't think you'll "get it wrong." There's rarely such a thing as a "bad" confrontation. Just by having the courage to do it you will grow ten feet in self-respect, and if you follow the guidelines in this chapter, there's no way you can fail. If you break down while you're saying these things to him, remind him that this is very painful and difficult for you and you need a few minutes to get yourself together. Then go back to what you need to say.

5. Yes, you have the right to confront him even if you're not married or engaged or haven't made any commitments to each other. Do any of those situations abrogate your right to confront anyone who tells you a significant lie? And do they mean that you don't have a basic right to be treated with respect and honesty? Of course not.

If you're like most women, you've probably spent a lot of your life doing everything you could to avoid anything resembling confrontation. I want to assure you that I know a lot of what you're going through and how ambivalent you are probably feeling. I know how anxious the idea of facing your lover makes you feel. But until you confront him with your feelings and let him know what you want, you will be stumbling around in the dark, trying to guess or intuit what's possible for the two of you. You won't have any solid sense of what's real or what to do next. More than anything else, an effective confrontation will ground your perceptions and decisions in reality instead of hopes and fears.

THE FORGIVENESS TRAP

At this point you may be wondering, Why can't I just forgive him and get on with my life?

Forgiveness is tricky, and I think we should take a look at it.

As you'll find, I have some strong ideas that may fly in the face of many things you've been taught. Forgiveness in response to injury has become almost a mandate, and some people may tell you, "Don't confront—just forgive." But I've found that forgiveness without confrontation is usually empty, and it's often the result of intense pressure.

If your partner is contrite and begging for your forgiveness, it's difficult not to give in to his fervent requests for absolution. "Please forgive me," he may plead. "It will never happen again. I could never hurt you that way again." It's hard to resist the delicious fantasy that everything will be wonderful, he'll never lie to you again, and the two of you will walk off into the sunset together once you forgive him. But reality doesn't work that way. You may feel better in the short term if you forgive him immediately, but the intense pain of his deceptions and betrayals will still be dammed up inside you.

That can be hard to remember when, in addition to his pleas, you also face the badgering of family members or friends who want to see the two of you stay together and don't know how to respond to your emotional upheaval. "Look how he's suffering," they may say. "Can't you find it in your heart to forgive him?" Suddenly you've become the villain of the piece. And in addition to all the other feelings you're struggling with, now you're supposed to feel guilty because you know how much must occur before you can even consider pardoning him. The other people in your life may add some fear to the mix by making catastrophic predictions about what will happen if you don't forgive him immediately. I'll show you how to deal with both his and other people's responses in the next chapters.

The concept of forgiveness, especially when it hasn't been earned by the person who has injured you, often contains a subtle subtext: "If you forgive me, then we can both pretend that what I did wasn't so bad." Or even more troubling, "Can't you just forgive and forget?"—which to me really means "Let's pretend it never happened."

Allison wondered why forgiveness wasn't sufficient to heal her deep wounds of betrayal:

I've learned that forgiveness is very powerful. Why do I have to do all this other stuff? He says he's genuinely sorry and he's really learned his lesson and I'm working hard on forgiving him—why isn't that enough?

I told Allison that what she was suggesting was not enough because quick forgiveness, in many cases, actually gives the liar more license to lie. From his perspective, he can do what he wants, and if he gets caught, you may be upset, but ultimately you will forgive him. So his lies haven't cost him very much, and he has no burning reason to stop. Here are some questions about forgiveness that helped Allison put the issue into perspective. I'd like you to go through this list yourself before you rush to forgive prematurely:

- If you forgive him right away, why does he need to take any personal responsibility for lying to you?
- If you forgive right away, how do you work through your rage and your grief?
- If you forgive him, what kind of a message does that give him?
- Shouldn't he have to do some of the work?

I urge you to do the work in this half of the book before you even think about forgiving him. Forgiveness, if you choose it, should come only after you explore your true feelings and attitudes and after you decide what you ultimately want from the relationship. It should not be the result of pressure from him, other people, religion, or society.

CONFRONTATION, STEP BY STEP

Now it's time to learn how to bring your feelings and wishes to the table in a safe, clear way. Make a commitment to do this as soon as possible. You'll find, as almost every woman does, that the doing is much less scary than the anticipation.

First you'll need to decide on the method of confrontation that feels the most comfortable for you, whether it be in person or written. Because confrontation is so anxiety-laden, it's a good idea to write out what you want to say. Then you can either give the letter to your lover or read it aloud to him. Facing him without something prepared is not a good idea, no matter how articulate you may be, because it's highly likely that your nervousness and discomfort will drive the things you want to say right out of your head.

If, like Anne, you discover a major lie while your partner is at work, please resist the impulse to rush to the phone and confront him then and there. You can't put confrontation ahead of the work in the last chapter, and you don't have the tools yet. Remember, too, that the telephone is the worst device for confronting someone. It's cold and impersonal, and the other person can always hang up on you.

If you are in some sort of therapy, you may want your therapist to help prepare you for your confrontation.

Timing is important here. You need to schedule with your partner a time when you will both be physically and emotionally available to talk with a minimum of distractions. That means taking the phone off the hook and sending children to friends or relatives if possible. I want you to make the decisions about time and place—it's part of being proactive on your own behalf.

Once you have chosen the time, the place, and the method, you're ready to begin.

Your confrontation needs to start with getting an agreement from your partner. Say to him:

I'm ready to talk about what happened. This isn't easy for either of us, but I have some things to say and I would like you to agree to hear me out and not interrupt or contradict me. When I'm done, you can have all the time you want to respond and I promise to hear you out as well. Are you willing to do that?

Ninety-nine times out of a hundred, he'll say yes. If he doesn't, say, "Is there another time we can schedule when you will be willing to do that?" Don't proceed until you have that agreement. Even with it, you may still find that he will interrupt you, but you can remind him of his agreement. Without it, you're likely to have chaos.

THE THREE CORNERSTONES OF CONFRONTATION

Now, gather your thoughts and your courage. Structure what you are going to tell him using these three basic points as your guides:

1. This is what I know.
2. This is how it makes me feel.
3. This is what I want from you now.

Even though it may be tempting, your goal is not to insult, demean, or purposely antagonize him. You want, instead, to let him see where he stands with you at this moment, laying out the situation point by point.

POINT 1: THIS IS WHAT I KNOW

For both you and your lover, this is the foundation of the problem—the solid evidence of the lying. If you only have suspicions and speculations, you are not ready to confront him. Please feel free to continue reading this chapter, but be sure to see the discussion on suspicion and jealousy in Chapter 10. It will help guide you toward the skills you'll need to assess your relationship.

When you have solid evidence, whether he admits his lies or is still denying that he lied to you, the confrontation will allow you to evaluate his capacity to face his actions and take responsibility for them.

If the lies have accumulated over months and years, you may have a long list of incidents in mind. Or you may have one major shocking event—one moment of seeing him kissing another woman, an alarming phone call from your bank, a love letter to someone else, a document from his past that contradicts important information he's given you about himself.

Make a list containing the following items:

- This is what I saw.
- This is what I've been told.

- Here are the contradictions between what you told me and what I've discovered.

Be specific. If some of the incidents are old, let him know that you are talking about them now because even though you may have talked about these things before, you don't really feel any resolution.

This list is a valuable way of staying connected with the objective truth of the situation as it stands right now. He may try to deny or minimize the facts, but this, in black-and-white, is what happened. This is what you know.

Now, Practice

If the discovery is relatively recent and mainly involves one major lie, as it did for Jan when she discovered a prior marriage her husband hadn't told her about, this first step is a little easier.

Jan and Bill wanted to stay together, but Jan was still reeling from her discovery that Bill had lied to her about something so important. She realized that she had no idea how to handle the situation so they could work toward a resolution. Jan was eager to express her feelings and desires to Bill, but like many people, she just didn't have the words.

To start, we rehearsed point 1 until Jan felt comfortable. It's a good idea for you to rehearse these approaches out loud as well. New communication skills and new behavior may feel stiff and awkward at first, but they always get more comfortable as you use them.

First Jan practiced letting Bill know when and where she wanted to talk to him. Then she went over asking him to hear her out and not interrupt. For point 1, here is what she decided to say:

Bill, you know I love you and I think we can get past this, but I need to talk to you about the lying and how I feel about it. First of all, here's what I know. You decided, for whatever reason, to keep a piece of information from me that I had a right to know about. Then when I asked you about it, you compounded the first lie with a second one. I had to find out the truth by reading a loan application. Those are the facts. But then your explanation was such a soap opera that at this point I don't know what to believe.

By beginning with two positive statements, one loving and one optimistic, Jan created an atmosphere in which Bill would feel less threatened and defensive—and therefore far more able to hear what she was saying. Then, like Sgt. Joe Friday on the old show *Dragnet*, she delivered "just the facts," without any emoting. I encourage you to use, as Jan did, the words *lies* and *lying* instead of softer terms like *shading the truth, falsehoods, fibs,* or any other euphemisms. A lie is what it was and is. No amount of tiptoeing around it will change that.

Staying Focused

If you've been putting up with his lying for a long time and you have a list that seems to go on forever, you don't have to bury him under a minutely detailed replay of every lie he's ever told you. Kathy and David had a far more tenuous relationship than Jan and Bill, and Kathy wasn't at all sure she was going to stay with David. But she was determined to give it her all, so that if she did decide to end the marriage, she'd know that she had given him every chance.

When we talked about confrontation, Kathy said she didn't know where to start, because there had been so many lies, and she had already let him know each time she caught him in one. But each time she had faced him, either she had been furious and David had been apologetic and full of promises, or it had been a chaotic exchange of attacks and counterattacks.

I told Kathy that none of what they'd been doing came close to a structured confrontation, and she agreed. I suggested she explain that to David as the reason she needed to talk to him about these events again.

Here's some of what Kathy and I worked out for her to say to David. If there have been lots of lies in your relationship, you can change the details to fit your situation, but the basic structure will work for you:

David, I know we've talked about these things before, but I need to go over them in a calmer way with you and see if there's a possibility of salvaging our relationship. Here's what I know for sure. I know that you have lied to me about money. I know that you forged my signature on a credit-card application. I know that you failed to tell me the IRS was after you. I know that you have lied to me about your drinking and about attending meetings.

It's important in this first step to stay focused, as Kathy did, on the lies and not to bring up every grievance you may have about the relationship. Also, notice again that this is a basic outline of what you have seen, learned, discovered, and know, not what you feel. That comes next.

POINT 2: THIS IS HOW YOUR LYING MAKES ME FEEL

Sad, terrified, betrayed, bewildered, hurt, furious, contemptuous: these are some of the most common feelings you have when you discover your lover's lies. But don't assume just because he's seen you crying or yelling or silently brooding that he's making the connection between what he did and where you are emotionally.

You are entitled to tell him your emotional truth—the link between his behavior and your emotional turmoil, in all its complexity and colors. At this point you may be saying, "But he knows how I feel—why do I have to tell him again?" He may know some of what you feel, but he's very focused on his own survival right now, and chances are he's not as aware of what's going on with you as you think. He may see the sadness but not the rage or vice versa. And your sense of betrayal, of feeling tricked and insulted, may be invisible to him.

Remember, we're focusing on feelings, not thoughts. Most people don't distinguish between the two in everyday conversation. We tend to use "I feel" and "I think" almost interchangeably. Pick up a newspaper or watch the news on television and you'll quickly see how blurred the distinctions between thoughts and feelings are. Most of the time, ideas and beliefs are expressed as if they were feelings, and most of the time it doesn't matter. But confrontations are aimed at gaining clarity, so it's important for you to understand the difference.

How Are You Feeling?

In the early stages of my work with Helen, I asked her how Phil's lies about his on-line sex chats were making her feel. This is what she answered:

> *I don't have much trouble expressing my feelings. His lying makes me feel that he is a totally untrustworthy person and very weak. I feel that I have lost all respect for him, and I feel that maybe I should have left him a long time ago. I feel he's not going to change.*

I asked Helen if it would surprise her if I told her that she hadn't expressed one single feeling in those statements. She looked puzzled. I told her that feelings can almost always be described and expressed in one word, like the ones at the beginning of this section. As soon as you put the word *that* after the words *I feel*, you go right out of your emotions into your head. "I feel that he is a totally untrustworthy person" is a belief, not a feeling, as are the rest of the things Helen told me.

To help her understand this concept better, I did some sentence completion work with her. I repeated her statements as ideas and asked her to identify the feeling these ideas engendered:

1. When I think that Phil is a totally untrustworthy person, it makes me feel . . .
2. When I believe he is weak, it makes me feel . . .
3. When I think how much respect I have lost for him, it makes me feel . . .
4. When I think that maybe I should have left him long ago, it makes me feel . . .
5. When I believe he won't change, it makes me feel . . .

At first Helen had trouble with one-word answers, but soon she was able to express genuine feelings instead of ideas. Here were some of her answers to the above sentences: 1. angry; 2. contemptuous; 3. sad; 4. frightened; 5. discouraged.

Helen softened considerably as she began to connect with the feelings underneath the hard defenses she'd erected to protect herself against the ways Phil's behavior had affected her emotionally. I encouraged her to express these feelings to Phil as part of getting beyond the impasse they were in.

When you are ready to let your lover know your feelings, it's natural to worry that he will somehow use them against you, or see you as weak and vulnerable. You may be locked into the belief that it's better to stay angry than to be sad—at least anger has some power in it. But your healing depends on your ability to identify, express, and be comfortable with the full range of your feelings—even the ones that make you feel vulnerable. It's well worth the risk of being honest with him, and yourself.

POINT 3: THIS IS WHAT I WANT FROM YOU NOW

Setting conditions, the fourth of the five "C's," is the part that gives most people trouble. "I don't know what I want!" you're probably thinking. Of course you want an end to the lying, and of course you want to feel better. You might even be certain that what you want is to have him out of your life. And in some cases, that may be the healthiest thing that could happen. But because you are so torn right now, you probably have no idea what kind of relationship might be possible once you give him time to respond to this part of your confrontation. Here is where you define your limits, your wants, your expectations, and your nonnegotiable list of what is and isn't acceptable to you. These are your conditions.

A New Contract

The word to underline mentally is *now*. It is far too early to know what you want for the long term; that decision can only come over time. But you do have definite requirements today, and that is where you can begin. To start this phase, say to your partner:

Here's what I need from you in order to agree to stay in this relationship now. I'm not going to make any promises regarding the future at this point, but I'm willing to work with you to see if we can build a new relationship. This doesn't mean we can go back to the status quo. What we had can never be again, and that makes me really sad, but I'm willing to put a lot of effort into seeing what we can have together once some time has gone by.

Of course you will put these scripts in your own words, paraphrasing them any way you choose. They are meant only as guides to help you formulate what you want to say. But I do suggest that you cover the main points and not stray too far from this format. It's too easy to get sidetracked and go off on tangents when you don't have a clear idea of what to say.

Once you have done this brief preamble, you're ready to define the terms of your new contract. Regardless of what the lies have been about, here is the first thing to ask for: he must acknowledge and take personal responsibility for his actions and their effects. Taking personal responsibility means that he needs to admit:

- What he's done
- How much he's hurt you

If He's Lied about Other Women

This firm, no-compromise list of requirements is the foundation you'll need to begin thinking about whether it's possible to continue as a couple. It may mean that your lover will have to take actions that are complicated, like removing an employee he's been involved with, and it will definitely mean committing your joint resources to healing as a top priority. But every item on this list is essential. Consider these actions to be nonnegotiable:

1. He must immediately end all contact with her (or them).
2. He must enter into some form of therapy or counseling for himself, and the two of you need couples counseling.
3. He must recommit to a monogamous relationship.
4. He must be willing to work actively with you to build a new relationship based on truth and personal integrity. In short, *no more lying.*

Here's how Allison expressed these requirements to Scott:

I told him I'd call him when I felt ready to talk, and about five days after he moved to the motel I felt stronger, so I asked him to come over after the kids were in bed. I told him that I wasn't ready to give up but that I wasn't ready to say, "Sure, everything's going to work out" either. I did the "This is what I know" and "This is what I feel." I got through it OK—I was pretty teary, but that didn't matter. Then I said, "Here's what I want from you right now. I want you to acknowledge how terribly you've hurt me and how what we had together is forever changed. I want you to say straight out that you've slept with another woman. The woman you've been seeing can't continue to work for you, and I want your promise that you won't see her again. You know I'm in therapy, and you need to do the same. And don't say we can't afford it, because our insurance will cover a lot of it, and if we need to we'll dip into savings. I consider this the most important thing in our lives right now. I also want you to know that there must be an end to lying and deceiving me—I deserve better than that."

Questions Best Left Unasked
You'll notice that when Allison was telling Scott what she wanted from him, at no point did she ask him to describe every detail of the affair in living Technicolor. And I don't want you to do that either. In fact, it's a lot healthier for you if he doesn't go into detail, no matter how curious you may be. It's a great temptation to ask such questions as:

- What does she have that I don't have?
- Is she better in bed than I am?
- What did she do for you that I won't do?
- Is she prettier/younger/smarter/sexier?

You don't need the answers to those questions, and it's pretty masochistic to press him about them.

Other useless questions women usually ask at a time like this are:

- Why did you do it?
- How could you do that to me?

Even if you could get valid answers, which you can't, what difference would it make if you knew why? It won't change what happened or how you feel about it. Sometimes an affair is a symptom of a troubled relationship, and at other times it's nothing more complicated than the manifestation of a need for someone new and different. There could be a hundred different answers for why he chose to be unfaithful to you, and he probably doesn't know why himself. Stay focused on the major point: what do you want from him now? Don't get sidetracked by an overly emotional inquisition about the sexual prowess of other women, or the size of their breasts, or what might have been going on in his unconscious. That's a no-win scenario for you, and it will only keep your wounds open and bleeding.

Money Lies

If the most serious of his lies have been in the financial arena, your want list will have some similarities to the one we saw above, as well as several differences. Again, he must take personal responsibility for his behavior, acknowledge that he has lied to you, and acknowledge how much he has hurt you. He must also agree to the following:

1: To make you a full and informed partner in all financial decisions that involve expenditures over an amount you can both agree on. If money is tight, I would suggest $100. If you're financially comfortable, $500 is appropriate.
2: Regular meetings at least twice a month to go over your finances together and to inform each other of what money is coming in, what needs to be budgeted for, and what you will be able to save.
3: Full disclosure of all investments, assets, loans, or gifts to relatives or friends.
4: Full disclosure of all debts, liens, attachments, bankruptcies, and delinquent alimony or child-support payments.

5: If his lies have created financial chaos and you are close to bankruptcy or have already had to file, then in addition to all of the above requirements, he must agree to turn money matters over to a professional such as an accountant, money manager, or financial consultant. If there is no money available for such professional services, there are organizations that will work with you to consolidate your debts and set up budgets and payment plans. You can start by calling Debtors Anonymous and asking them for a referral. Knowing these facts will make you feel far more secure that what you're asking for is realistic.

6: No more lies.

I realize that these "requests" may sound pretty militant and even abrasive to you, especially if you've been somewhat passive about financial matters in the past. But if you examine them closely, you'll realize that they are both reasonable and fair. You can't have any peace of mind if you're constantly in the dark about what your partner is doing with money. And avoiding the jolts to your nervous system when a check bounces or you find, as Diane did, that he's invested your savings in some scheme you know too little about, or that the IRS is after him, as Kathy learned, is more important than trying to avoid sounding more forceful than usual.

Getting Past the Pessimism

Diane was drowning in Ben's lies about money, yet she was quite taken aback when I suggested to her that Ben's reckless and deceptive behavior was very much like that of a compulsive gambler and that therapy by itself wasn't going to be enough. He needed to recognize that his behavior with money was out of control and that he could no longer make unilateral decisions about finances.

Diane was pessimistic about how Ben would react when she confronted him, and she was certain that he wouldn't agree to any of her terms:

It won't do any good to confront him. He's had a free rein on the spending for as long as we've been married, and like a schmuck I've gone along with it to keep the peace. Also, I didn't want to show him I didn't have faith in him. I thought a good, supportive wife is supposed to encourage her husband. I realize that I've just been encouraging him to be reckless and irresponsible. Now I'm doing a complete one-eighty and saying "No—I really didn't have any faith in you. In fact, you've been scaring me to death." I just know he won't agree to any of these demands. He won't let me or anyone else manage the money. He'll see it as a threat to his manhood and his right to make his own decisions, no matter how crazy and destructive they are.

"So what's your alternative?" I asked. "You can't go on the way you've been. Even if you manage to pull out of this disaster, his grandiosity and need to be the big shot will create another one." Diane nodded sadly in agreement.

I told Diane that she might well be right in her assessment of how Ben would react to her new behavior. Some men will resist change with every molecule of their bodies and say you're emasculating them when you attempt to set limits and ask for what you want. But you won't know until you try. You have a lot more leverage than you think—don't be afraid to use it. Chances are he doesn't want to lose you. And if continuing to spend recklessly is more important to him than restoring your peace of mind and rebuilding your relationship, it's better to find out sooner than later.

Diane had the same options that are available to any woman who learns of her partner's lying:

- Leave in anger without ever knowing if positive change could have occurred.
- Continue in an intolerable situation, never knowing when the next lie or betrayal will occur and with your fears running the show.
- Confront him appropriately and let his responses indicate what is possible for you in the future with this man.

Which do you think is best?

Lies about Addictions

It is a given that if your lover is addicted to drugs or alcohol and is not receiving treatment, your life with him has been one lie after another. When you confront a man who has an addiction, you need, of course, to do it at a time when he is lucid and not under the influence. Again, you will tell him what you know and how it makes you feel, but the requirements under "This is what I want from you now" will have some significant additions.

1: He must enter the appropriate Twelve Step program immediately and attend meetings regularly as a condition of your agreeing to stay in the relationship for the moment. *Nothing else is acceptable*—not therapy, not meditating, not astrology, not exercising more, and not the determination to have more willpower. All these things are fine, but they won't control the addiction. If he won't go into a Twelve Step program, or if he enters one primarily to appease you and then drops out after a few meetings, there is little chance that your relationship can survive, and even less chance that you will survive living with an addicted man. Psychotherapy has proven ineffective for most addictions. You may want to try it later on, but remember that he has to be clean and sober for at least three months before starting any kind of therapy.

2: In addition to what you require him to do, it's essential for your own well-being that you enter a program such as Al-Anon or Nar-Anon for the partners of addicts. The world of addiction is fraught with misconceptions and confusion. Without the caring support of your own program, it's easy to step on emotional land mines as you struggle to cope with something you simply don't know how to handle. You will learn a lot about yourself in such programs, and I urge you to get into one, even if you decide to end the relationship.

Other Lies, Other Arenas

Sex, money, and addiction may be the subjects that most men lie about; they're usually the ones that cause the most emotional chaos. Often you'll find that the man in your life is lying about more than one of those topics. And he may well lie about others. You've seen scenarios in this book in which men lie to women about their past, their family history, and about wives they don't want their current partners to know about. The details of your case may be unique. But whatever the subject of the lie, you need to confront him the same way.

Remember that you'll always want him to acknowledge that he's lied and that he's deceived and hurt you. You want an end to the lying, and you want to be respected enough to be told the truth about his past and present if there's to be any chance of a future.

Confrontation empowers you. You will come out of it knowing that you have found the courage to tell your truth and to ask for what you want. Taking action, and not just waiting to react to what he says and does, will increase your self-respect immeasurably. It will forever change the dynamics of a relationship for the better. And equally important, confrontation will give you enough clarity about your lover and your relationship that you can make sound, thoughtful decisions about where to go from here.

9

Handling His Responses

In a perfect world, you would confront your lover, he would quietly and thoughtfully listen to everything you have to say, and he would then respond with, "I'm so sorry—I never meant to hurt you. I know I've been a damn fool and I will do anything you ask to work with you toward building a new and better relationship free from lies. I take full responsibility for everything I've done and I want to change. I will go to therapy, couples counseling, anything you want. You can talk to me about this whenever you need to and I will listen to you and not get defensive. I will agree to all your requirements—I find them fair and reasonable. Is there anything else you need from me now?" Wouldn't that be wonderful? But the world is not perfect and neither is he—or you. Unfortunately, his responses rarely come close to the ideal.

But that doesn't mean you should in any way underestimate the power of your confrontation. You've set the tone for a new kind of dialogue and negotiation that will lead you toward a fresh start. It's likely that he has never heard you express yourself in such a focused, direct manner, and by doing so, you've created the best possible atmosphere for the important work that lies ahead for both of you.

THE OTHER HALF OF CONFRONTATION

You've said your piece. You've told him what you know and what you want from him. Now you need to stand firm and stay committed to the honesty, openness, and respect you want and deserve as you deal with the second part of confrontation—your partner's responses.

Chances are, your lover will feel even more cornered when you confront him than he did when you first found out about his lying. Most men will do almost anything to avoid looking bad. He's going to feel guilty, vulnerable, embarrassed, and even humiliated. He'll have a tough time with this kind of exchange, and being confronted this directly is not exactly his idea of fun. He'll be very off balance, and he may be more concerned with regaining his footing than responding to what you've said. As a result, he may resort to tactics similar to the ones he used when you first found out about his lies, with some new wrinkles. He may once again:

- Try to minimize his behavior
- Blame you or others for his behavior
- Work on your sympathies

He may now also:

- Expect automatic amnesty because he's apologized
- Quietly refuse to honor some or all of your requirements
- Get angry with you for making so many demands on him and accuse you of trying to control him

And in a few instances, if he has used denial in the past, he may continue to use it now, even in the face of overwhelming evidence.

But this time you are going to be very different from the way you were when you discovered that he'd been lying to you. Don't forget that you carry with you the clarity you've gained by doing the hard work of planning and presenting the confrontation to your partner. You have identified what you want, and because you've laid a lot of groundwork, you'll find that the old explanations won't sound the same to you. The old emotional ploys won't move you into the familiar mists that have confused you in the past. You're different now—awake in a new way to both the impact of his past lies and what the future may hold. You may feel scared or shaky, but you are stronger.

NEW COMMUNICATION SKILLS

Regardless of what techniques he uses, when it's your partner's turn to respond to your confrontation, it's not enough that you just close your mouth and open your ears. It's essential that you hear him accurately and not gloss over any ambiguous or confusing responses he makes.

To help you do this, I want you to learn two simple techniques: clarifying and paraphrasing. Clarifying will help you prevent false assumptions and misperceptions. Some examples of clarifying questions are:

- I'm not sure I understood what you just said. Did you mean . . . ?
- Are you saying that . . . ?
- Could you help me understand what you mean?

Paraphrasing involves playing back to your partner what he just said in your own words. Like clarifying, it can also clear up a lot of misunderstandings as well as letting the other person know they've been heard. When you use paraphrasing, you begin sentences like:

- Let me get this straight . . .
- So what you're saying is . . .
- If I hear you right . . .

Most of us are used to letting confusing statements go by without questioning them. "I wonder what he really means by that," you think, without asking him to explain. By focusing closely on what he's saying and being determined to clarify whatever you don't fully understand, you'll be listening actively.

I know it takes a lot of energy to listen this intently, but your listening will ground you. It will lead you to what you need to know, and not incidentally, it will also keep your focus where it will do the most good—on him, instead of on you and your anxiety. When your focus is on how he's responding, you're automatically going to be less preoccupied with how scared or upset you may be.

Once you've practiced these techniques and made them a part of your repertoire, you're ready to deal with the specific maneuvers he may use to weave and dodge when he responds to you.

If the lying has been ongoing, you're familiar with his manipulations and understandably concerned that he'll get the best of you once again. If this is the first serious lie you've found out about, you're probably unsure of what he'll say and what to believe. In either case, I'm going to prepare you to deal with a variety of potential responses, which will enable you to show him that he must take you seriously and that you won't be swayed by any of the techniques that have worked for him in the past.

MINIMIZING: THE IT-WASN'T-SO-BAD RESPONSE

In the cosmic scheme of things, compared with wars, plagues, and weapons of mass destruction, what's really so bad about a little affair, or a few bounced checks, or an ex-wife he neglected to tell you about? At least that's what your lover would like you to believe as he tries to make the tremendous pain he's caused you look like a paper cut. He's not a serial killer, after all, and look at all the wonderful things he's done.

You may be so thrilled your lover has admitted to his lies instead of denying them that you eagerly pounce on the words "Yes, I did it" without paying enough attention to what he says next. It's important to watch out for responses that sound as if he's taking responsibility but that are actually evasive, aimed at placating you by minimizing his role in what he's done.

If the sexual arena is the one where he's been telling the most serious lies, he may attempt to use some typical excuse-laden rationalizing statements like the following:

- "Yes, I had an affair. It just happened." (I had nothing to do with it—we somehow mysteriously ended up in bed together.)
- "Yes, I slept with her, but I was drunk." (The liquor excuse.)
- "Yes, I know I hurt you. I don't know what got into me. I must have been out of my mind." (The insanity defense.)
- "It had nothing to do with you." (You weren't supposed to find out. I figured that what you didn't know wouldn't hurt you.)

If he uses phrases like these in an attempt to minimize the seriousness of what he did, you need to say:

"What I want from you is a clear acknowledgment that one, you were sexually intimate with another woman; two, you betrayed me; three, you lied to me; four, you have hurt me terribly and aren't fully aware of how much."

Don't be afraid to coach him and ask him to repeat these statements back to you in his own words. They are what he needs to say to you without excuses and without disclaimers. These phrases are clear and truthful, and you have every right to ask for them.

If the major lies were about financial issues, addiction, or other aspects of his life, watch out for minimizing statements like:

- "I don't know why you're making a federal case out of this."
- "You're overreacting."
- "Everybody does it. Everybody drinks/uses cocaine/has affairs/gets overdrawn at the bank/lies about their past."

According to the situation, tell him that what you need to hear him say are things like:

- "I admit I've been financially reckless/deceptive/irresponsible."
- "I admit I lied about my past."

- "I admit I'm using alcohol/drugs heavily."
- "I admit I have not been attending meetings/therapy regularly."

Then you need to ask him to follow his acknowledgment of what he's done with an acknowledgment that he's lied to you and that he's hurt you deeply.

NO TIME FOR COMEDY

As you listen to your lover in this early phase of his responses, you need to feel confident that he's taking you and your requests seriously. This is no time for joking around, so watch out for phrases designed to minimize his behavior and win you over with their supposed cuteness.

Randy had always been able to charm his way out of most of the conflicts that he and Anne had over the years, so it was natural for him to assume that this would work for him again:

When I told him the first thing I wanted from him was to take personal responsibility for the affair and to validate that he'd hurt me deeply, he said that was perfectly understandable. But instead of saying it like a grown-up, he got that mischievous look that he knows melts my heart and put his head down and said, "I've been a very bad boy." I guess that was his idea of lightening things up, but all it did was make me furious. I told him he was lucky I let him live after that, and no, he hadn't been a bad boy— he'd been a shitty man, and he'd better start taking me seriously!

On the defensive, and with so much at stake, Randy understandably fell back on a strategy that had worked for him in the past—playing the naughty but contrite little boy. But he'd seriously underestimated how much stronger Anne was now, not to mention the depth of her anger. When she wouldn't let him get away with this ploy, he settled down and began to communicate with her in a far more appropriate way.

Other examples of attempts to make light of a serious situation include:

- "The devil made me do it."
- "There must have been a full moon."
- "You know how men are."
- "Well—it could be worse. I could be Jack the Ripper."

If he uses language like this, let him know that you understand how awkward and uncomfortable all this is for him but that he's only making things worse by trying to be funny. If an attempt at playfulness begins to color his need for a full acknowledgment of what he's done, it's up to you to make it clear that you're not playing and he shouldn't be either.

SHIFTING THE BLAME

Unless he's really dense, he probably knows by the tone of your confrontation that a blatant attempt to shift the blame for his bad behavior onto you is not going to get very far. But that doesn't mean that he won't try to get himself off the hook by using the old you-drove-me-to-it response. It may be more subtle, and it may come hand in hand with the appearance of taking responsibility, but you still need to watch out for blame-shifting phrases like:

- "I only did it because you . . ."
- "If you were more _____, I never would have needed to . . ."
- "I had to. You were just too . . ."

In the long form, these blame-shifting phrases translate to such statements as:

- "Yes, I had an affair, but you've got to look at your role too. I just didn't feel understood. You're always so busy and involved in your work/the new baby/helping your mother/your charities. . . ."
- "Yes, I lied about my drinking, but you're such a nag—it's the only pleasure I have."
- "Yes, I lied about making the investment, and I know you're really upset, but I did it for us. You're just so damned timid

and you get so hysterical about money—if it was up to you
we'd never do anything that has a chance at making a
killing."

Faced with an onslaught of blame from someone we're close
to, we often allow self-doubt to take hold and we crumble a little. In
the past, his use of blame may have been enough to prompt an automatic retreat for you, and you may still have a tendency to do that.
Nobody changes overnight. We're all vulnerable to charges that
we're not sexy or smart or nurturing enough and that our character
flaws caused him to resort to lying. There may even be some truth
in what he's saying. But you must hold on to this truism: Nothing
you are or do justifies his lying to you.

So this time I want you to promise yourself that you're not
going to play the blame game. You're going to handle his blaming
responses with empowering, nondefensive responses of your own.
I realize that many of these statements sound much stronger than
you may be feeling—that's natural. But the more you learn to
respond in these ways, the sooner your self-confidence will catch
up to your brave words. Answer his rationalizations with any or all
of the following:

- "This is about your lying, it's not about my shortcomings."
- "Lying was your choice and your decision."
- "You had plenty of other options, including talking to me
  about what was bothering you so that we could have
  looked for a solution together."
- "I am not willing to take the responsibility for your
  behavior."

Practice these statements whenever you can. Notice how
grounded they make you feel. Notice, too, that there is nothing
belligerent or abrasive about them. They are the way you set your
boundaries and make clear what you will and won't be responsible for.

THE ARTFUL DODGER

One of the most frustrating things to observe is the sight of a grown man reverting to the schoolboy's tactics of blaming someone else for his misdeeds instead of facing the consequences of his actions.

Scott initially responded to Allison's confrontation with what seemed like a willingness to take full responsibility for his affair, but then he subtly switched gears and attempted to place some of the blame on the other woman:

He said pretty much what I was asking for, but then he came out with "I know what I did was wrong, but she just wouldn't let up. She came after me with everything she had." In the past I would have bought into what he was saying, but this time I was able to hold my ground. I used paraphrasing and clarifying, and I said, "OK—let me see if I understood you accurately. Are you saying that she seduced you and you had no choice but to go along with it? That makes me really uncomfortable, Scott, because it sounds like you're not taking responsibility for your own decisions."

When this kind of finger-pointing comes up, you need to play his statements back to him as Allison did and let him know that (1) you appreciate his going through this with you and (2) no matter how seductive the other person may have been, it was his decision to let himself get seduced.

Obviously it takes two people to have an affair, and certainly a woman who sleeps with a married man is making her own less than healthy choices, but that did not eclipse Scott's need to take full responsibility for his choice, which resulted in enormous pain for his wife. With Allison's insistence, Scott was able to acknowledge this and agreed to enter counseling. I referred him to a colleague of mine. Only time will tell if Scott and Allison will make it together, but with Scott's willingness to change and Allison's clear limit-setting, I think they have a good chance.

If he blames others for his lies about money, substance abuse, or anything else, keep reminding him that he's an adult with the ability to make choices. Unfortunately, he made the wrong ones, regardless of the pressure other people may have put on him to spend, drink, stay out till all hours, or make a crazy investment.

Confrontation is not about blaming. Blaming defeats the purpose and often the chance of any real resolution. Remember, what you accept, you teach. If you accept the blame for what he's done, you are teaching him how to get you to back off whenever he gets caught in a lie. Conversely, when his blaming doesn't have the expected results, he may just drop it entirely and even be willing to accept the responsibility for his actions.

WORKING ON YOUR SYMPATHIES

You're probably all too familiar with the type of response your partner may come up with if he's an expert at becoming pathetic when he feels threatened. In response to your confrontation, he may ignore your requirements and instead cry, plead, beg, get openly depressed, or even threaten to hurt himself if you don't immediately promise to stay with him forever. He may say things like:

- "You know I can't live without you."
- "This is killing me."
- "Yes I lied to you, but that doesn't make me a monster. How can you degrade me like this?"
- "I'm getting really depressed."
- "I've never felt so awful about anything in my life."

On cue, you're supposed to turn to jelly, stop any attempt at resolving the crisis, and fall into his arms. At least that's the scenario he has in mind, especially if this kind of strategy has been successful for him before. Keep in mind that your lover may not be aware of how manipulative he's being—this may be a habitual response for him that's worked well in the past to keep him out of trouble.

Even more upsetting is to see a man who is normally not very emotional suddenly become this upset. Your first impulse may be to comfort him and forget about what you're trying to accomplish. Resist it. Instead, answer him with gentle but firm reminders such as:

- "I can see how this is upsetting you. But we won't get anywhere unless you respond to my specific requirements."
- "I'm sorry you're upset, but I've been very upset too. Let's deal with what I'm asking of you, because that will get us unstuck."

I'VE SAID I'M SORRY—ISN'T THAT ENOUGH?

For many men, the operative equation is Confession equals Absolution. It's not easy for people to acknowledge that they've lied or to apologize for it, and they want full credit for the effort. Too often, though, they want their acknowledgment to be the end point of the crisis.

In Chapter 2 you saw examples of men confessing their lies and in some instances feeling that their confessions gave them permission to keep on lying. David was a master at not delivering on his promises after innumerable apologies and confessions. Before Kathy did her confrontation, she asked me what would be different this time, even with more structure and more specific requirements.

I asked her to imagine some of the things that David would say in his attempt to get immediate absolution. Here's what she came up with:

- "I'm sorry, I did it, I love you, I'll never do it again. Can we drop it now?"
- "What do you want from me? Sackcloth and ashes?"
- "What can I say after I say I'm sorry?"

I told Kathy these were pretty typical maneuvers aimed at making her feel guilty for being so hard on him. I asked her to think through some responses to them. They included:

David, you don't need to say anything. What you need is to do certain things, which I've outlined to you. You also need to stop whining and acting like such a martyr. I'm the injured party here, and you know from the program that you need to make amends—not just keep saying how sorry you are. In the past I've gone along with your apologies and confessions, but that's not going to happen anymore. They're just words, and unless they're followed by some consistent, obvious behavioral changes, all the I'm-sorries in the world don't mean diddly. I want this to work out, if possible, and I'm willing to give this some time, but I can't wait indefinitely. The ball is really in your court now.

"Sounds pretty good to me," I said.

To have any hope of rebuilding your relationship, you'll have to hold your partner to a much higher standard. You'll need proof of his intent to change—a kind of down payment on his promises. You need action, not just words, even when the words seem to be genuine and the emotions behind them true.

"YES, BUT . . ."

What if he acknowledges that he's deceived and betrayed you, says he's ready to take personal responsibility, commits to honesty, and swears never to lie to you again—but only agrees to some of your requirements. He may say he's willing to do everything except go to counseling, either alone or with you. Or he may agree to be more open about money but resist going to a financial adviser, assuring you that he can manage things just fine without outside advice. Then what?

It's tempting to back down when he agrees to most of what you're asking for, and I know you're afraid of looking tyrannical if you insist that he agree to all the items on your "This is what I want from you now" list. So here are some suggestions about how to respond if he's only willing to go along with some of the things you're asking for:

- If he's cheated on you sexually, there is nothing on your list of requirements that is unreasonable or overly militant. You cannot get on solid ground unless he agrees to all the items on your list. If he agrees to all the others but balks at getting professional help, don't back down. Professional help doesn't mean spending thousands of dollars and seeing someone for ten years. It can be short-term crisis-oriented intervention, but you will need someone to give you some communication and behavioral guidelines. He also needs to work on whatever it was in him that made him choose to have an affair so that he can develop enough self-awareness to make healthier choices in the future. I strongly suggest you tell him that therapy is not negotiable.
- If substance abuse is involved, regular attendance in a Twelve Step program is also not negotiable. Only he can decide to go, but if he doesn't, you will not stay.
- With money issues, you can agree to put going to a credit counselor off for a little while unless you are severely in debt and see no way out of it. You can agree to a thirty-day probationary period during which time you will have a chance to see if he's been able to change his attitudes and behavior with money. If he insists on maintaining total control without involving you in major money decisions, you're right back where you were. At that point, outside guidance is a must.

Remember, you have a lot of leverage right now. Don't be afraid to hang tough as he's trying to squirm out of doing unpleasant things like taking an honest look at himself.

RESPONDING WITH ANGER

In the worst-case scenario, your lover will use your confrontation as justification to attack you and get you to back off. Remember, he's going to feel threatened by the change in you, and if he has a quick temper and explodes easily, you will need to prepare yourself.

Ben initially got angrier than Diane had ever seen him when she set out her requirements about how money was to be handled in the future:

He has a strong voice anyway, but this time he was really screaming at me. He said that he'd give money to his daughter if he wanted to and that neither I nor any "goddamn pencil pusher credit counselor" was going to tell him what he could and couldn't do with his money.

I don't know where I got the guts, but I did what we'd practiced and told him I wouldn't listen to him until he calmed down. Then I walked out of the room. He looked totally stunned—I'd never done that before. I wish I could say I felt completely calm and confident but I didn't. I was scared shitless. My heart was pounding and I had no idea what was going to happen—I was in totally unfamiliar waters.

Diane had hit a nerve with Ben, who felt extremely threatened by the idea that he would not be in total control of the finances any longer. As a result, he exploded and tried to intimidate her.

I assured Diane that new behavior is never comfortable, for the very reasons she identified: it's unfamiliar, and we don't know what will happen next. If Diane had taken the path of least resistance and done what she had done in the past, which was to let Ben off the hook, she undoubtedly would have felt better in the short run because she would have known what was coming. Ben would have calmed down immediately, and they would have reverted to their old patterns.

But Diane was not about to betray herself and all the work we had done together. She decided, as you must decide whenever you try out new behavior, to tolerate the discomfort, knowing that it's the sign that you're doing it right. The old unhealthy behavior is always more comfortable. New, effective, strong behavior is always going to throw you off balance. But if you hang in there, you will set in motion the changes that must take place.

Shortly after Diane walked away from Ben's anger, he followed her and agreed to talk with her in a more rational way.

When Ben saw that Diane really meant business this time, he had the good sense to realize that he had a lot to lose by continuing to insist on controlling the money, especially with his track record. He finally agreed to all the nonnegotiable items on her list.

But not every angry man will calm down and become reasonable because you hold the line, and it would be irresponsible of me to suggest that they will. If he's prone to temper tantrums, you may not even get through what you want to say before he goes ballistic. If he starts to yell or bawl you out for having the nerve to make so many demands on him or for not having the good sense to drop the whole matter, there's not much you can do other than refuse to continue until he quiets down.

If that doesn't work, I strongly advise you to do what Diane did: say something like "I'm not willing to be yelled at" and walk away. I know you're going to feel very frustrated and hopeless at this point and I don't blame you. If you let him know that you won't allow him to yell or scream at you and he then escalates rather than diminishes his verbal and emotional assault on you, you need to ask yourself the following questions:

- What kind of future can you have with a man who lies to you and won't listen to you?
- What kind of future can you have with a man who lies to you and then needs to intimidate you when you try to do something about it?
- What kind of future can you have with a man who lies to you and doesn't respect you?
- What kind of future can you have with a man who lies to you and refuses to work with you toward a healthier relationship?

The answer to all of these questions is, sadly, none.

A Word of Warning

Don't confront a man you think could become physically violent. If he has physically assaulted you in any way, you should have left him when that occurred. If you're still with a man who has hit you before, and

**you fear he may hit you again, his lying is the least of
your worries. You need counseling immediately so
that you don't end up a statistic.**

WHEN HIS ONLY RESPONSE IS DENIAL

Some men (not most by any means), even in the face of solid evidence, will continue to deny they've done any of the things you
have discovered.

You can't force your partner to acknowledge his lies. That's a
step he has to come to on his own. I have no problem with you,
giving him a brief period of time, say a day or two, to get there.
But the issue of his taking personal responsibility has to be a deal
breaker. It's the difference between starting a healthy dialogue
between you as you work toward change, and the sad, difficult
truth that you will have to make a choice between your relationship and your emotional well-being.

If his response to being confronted is to continue to deny
everything, then he has really made the decision for you. He has
decided that there will be no honesty or respect in your relationship. And without those two essential ingredients, there can be
no genuine emotional intimacy.

Your lover's responses to your confrontation give you the
most important information you'll ever have to help you make
the decision about whether this relationship can rise from the
ashes of deception and betrayal. But it will take time and
patience to get your answer.

Remember, nothing is etched in stone. A decision you make
today can always be changed if your partner reverts to his old
patterns or fails to make good on his commitments. As you enter
this new phase of your life, be reassured by the knowledge that
you can take all the time you need to become comfortable with
the changes in your lover, your relationship, and, most of all,
yourself.

10

If You Stay

If your lover has responded willingly to your requirements for rebuilding the relationship, there's obviously a sense of relief and even joy. You're at a crossroads, but perhaps you can begin again. You're also aware that your initial relief has to be tempered, because hope is now filtered through lingering pain, doubt, uncertainty, and the grief that comes with knowing that something dear to you has been lost. The bad news is that the easy, innocent trust you had before is gone and won't be back. The good news is that you may be able to replace it with a wiser, more honest kind of intimacy.

But few of us have the vaguest idea how to act in a relationship that has been riddled with lies, and the next weeks and months are critical. In this chapter, I'll give you the tools for returning to everyday life with your partner without falling back into old patterns—or walking into the traps that so often sabotage women as they work to regain their self-respect and dignity after they've been badly hurt. I'll also help you look realistically at how the relationship is doing over time, as you continue to consider what you want for the future. Remember, the only decision you need to make after a positive confrontation is that you are willing to give the relationship time to change. Only time can tell whether you and he will be able to reconnect and go on.

IT'S NOT ALL UP TO HIM

In the first few days after confrontation, you may believe that the bulk of your efforts are behind you. You've worked hard. You've been honest and brave. You've learned a lot of new communication skills. And now you'd like to be cut some slack. After all, he's the one who behaved badly and now has got to regain your trust. No matter what your flaws or shortcomings may be, you're the one who's been hurt, deceived, lied to, and emotionally devastated. At this point you may be wondering what more anyone can ask of you.

I'm sorry to have to tell you that your work doesn't end after confrontation. Your 50 percent of the rebuilding process involves a lot more than simply laying down the law and waiting for your lover to prove himself.

A few weeks after Randy had responded very positively to her confrontation, Anne saw how tempting it was to put the ball totally in Randy's court:

Things are really weird. We're tense around each other and really strained. He's nervous and guilty, and I get sarcastic a lot. I find myself wanting to say, "OK, you bastard. I've done all this work, now prove to me that you've changed. I'm waiting." I feel like the warden, and that's no way to be in a marriage.

"Nobody said it was going to be easy," I told Anne, "and one of the biggest mistakes many women make as they move past confrontation into a period of truce and evaluation is to sit back, try to nurse their wounds, watch for infractions, and wait for their partner to convince them that he's a different man now."

Like Anne, you may reason that your work is done. You've planted the seeds, and now you want to see what the flower looks like. Sitting back and waiting for him to assuage all your doubts and suspicions is tempting, but it's self-defeating. While he certainly has his work cut out for him, you need to participate actively in creating an atmosphere that will allow and encourage the relationship to evolve to a healthier plateau.

The most effective and healing way to do this is to continue to use and develop the communication skills you learned during the confrontation process and to add some new ones that I will show you. They'll steady and support you every step of the way.

WALKING ON EGGS

The tension and nervousness that Anne described are typical aftereffects of confrontation. The knowledge that so much has to change brings a disconcerting sense of tentativeness to your relationship. You used to be able to toss off comments without a thought and be loose and casual with each other. Now you're both walking on eggs, not sure how to regain any sense of the ease you used to have. It's as though, in light of what's happened, every word has new meaning. You're probably censoring almost everything you say, and both of you are straining to hear what's really being said and what's being hidden or withheld.

As Kathy described it:

We used to practically finish each other's sentences, but now we need subtitles. I don't know how to react to him, and I have no idea how to talk to him, so a lot of the time I just don't say anything. It's better than saying the wrong thing and hurting his feelings or starting a fight.

I told Kathy that while it might feel safer to tiptoe around and be extra polite, what she needed now was honesty more than caution. I asked her to remember how it felt when she finally told David how his lying affected her.

It felt like a ten-thousand-pound weight was lifted off my chest. It felt light and clean. I felt stronger and a lot less angry.

I told Kathy I wanted her to take a moment to reexperience those feelings of lightness and strength and to picture them as a cloud, or whatever image worked for her. I told her to lock that image into her mind and heart so that she could draw on it whenever she needed to.

"Remember what a relief it was to ask him questions to clarify what he meant and to express yourself clearly. Neither of you was mind reading or afraid to say what you meant. You took a risk, and so far it's paid off. That's what will help you stop walking on eggs with each other."

If you find yourself falling into patterns of watching everything you say or do, use the imagery of the lightness of truth to return you to the clarity you had during confrontation. In the coming days and weeks, bring the communication tools of clarifying and paraphrasing into your everyday life. It takes some discipline to break the obsessive patterns of stewing about everything you say and what he might have meant, but the rewards are worth it.

Express yourself directly, with sensitivity to his feelings but without fear. Listen carefully, then clarify and paraphrase his responses to be sure you understand. It's a new way of being with him. It will undoubtedly feel awkward at first, but it will become more comfortable as you practice—not only with him, but with other situations and people in your everyday life.

Of course you don't have to be "communicating brilliantly" every moment of your life. Nobody does. In the heat of emotion, it's very easy to forget everything you've learned and either attack or withdraw. But then it's up to you to get yourself back on track. And of course you don't have to paraphrase everything; there must be times when you're not working at this and let yourself just relax. But the more you practice these skills, the less tentative you will be with each other, and the more both of you will have a chance to end old patterns of evasion, confusion, and letting things slide.

You will find that even though these communication strategies feel somewhat mechanical at first, as you continue to use them, something quite wonderful will be happening internally. Knowing that you can draw on skills that will give you reliable information about what's happening in the relationship, you'll find that you have a heightened sense of confidence.

TRADING POWER PLAYS FOR EMPOWERMENT

A major impediment in your journey toward healing yourself and, if possible, your relationship is the lingering need to punish him.

After all, it seems that he's been in the driver's seat, he's been in control of the information, he's done what he wanted to do, and if you're staying, what has his bad behavior cost him? The desire to punish him can remain strong even after the apologies and the commitment to change that resulted from confrontation. As Allison put it:

I hope you're not suggesting that I'm supposed to go out of my way now to help him feel more comfortable. I don't want him to be comfortable—I want him to feel miserable.

I'm sure you can identify with Allison's reaction. There is a self-righteousness in her position that can feel delicious. Any woman who has been lied to knows how powerful and in control it feels to take this kind of stand. But it's an illusion. Punishing, like revenge, may bring a temporary shift in the balance of power, but it almost guarantees that the new relationship you are trying to build will not flourish.

You may not think you're having a problem with punishing, but it's such a typical part of a strained relationship that you'd have to be a saint to totally avoid it. Punishing behavior can take many forms—some subtle, some very aggressive. Most women find that at least one of the following examples sounds like a page from their postconfrontation life.

Punishing Behavior No. 1: Guilt-Tripping

This is the granddaddy of them all. You're the victim and he's the thoughtless pig who frittered away your savings or betrayed you with another woman, and you want to make very sure that he does plenty of mea culpas. I know you're all familiar with how guilt-tripping sounds, but it doesn't hurt to take another look at some old favorites:

- "You ruined our lives."
- "You ruined our marriage."
- "Look how miserable/depressed/nervous I am."
- "I hope you're happy now."
- "How dare you argue with me after what you did."

- "How are you going to make this up to me?"
- "I think you're the worst person on the face of the earth."
- "You ought to be ashamed of yourself."

Scott had agreed to every one of Allison's conditions, including entering therapy. But Allison was having an understandably hard time letting go of the need to keep punishing him:

I want him to suffer the way I did. Yes, I want him to feel guilty. Guilt is what will make him toe the line. Aren't you the one who talks about taking personal responsibility for our behavior? I don't want him to forget for a second what he's done! I want him to feel so lousy about it, he'll think long and hard the next time he's attracted to somebody else.

Maybe You Don't Really Want What You Think You Want
"And what's that going to do for you?" I asked. "If he has a conscience, don't worry—he feels plenty guilty. And if he doesn't have a conscience, you shouldn't be with him. Taking personal responsibility means acknowledging what we've done that's harmful and making the appropriate amends. As far as I can tell, Scott's doing just that. Let me be Scott for a minute and see if I can figure out how you'd like him to behave to prove to you he's 'guilty enough.'"

As Scott, I became hangdog and supplicating to an absurd degree:

"I'll never get over what I did to you—I will be your slave, I will cater to your every whim, I will beat myself with birch branches every morning before the sun comes up, I will never so much as smile at any other woman. Will that be enough, Oh lord and master?"

"Stop it!" Allison shrieked. "I can't stand it! He sounds like a total idiot—that's not what I want."

By taking Allison's punishment fantasies to an extreme degree, I was able to tap into the part of her which knew that what she thought she wanted was both irrational and self-defeating.

Susan: OK—then what do you want? Given a choice between making sure he grovels enough and rebuilding your marriage, which would you take?

Allison: You know the answer to that—I really do want us to make it. But I don't know . . . his guilt makes me feel safe. . . . But I know that's a myth because nobody wants to be around someone who constantly makes them feel bad about themselves.

Susan: You just discovered something very important. A lot of women believe that if he's guilty enough, he'll be too miserable to ever hurt them again. But in reality, you're not safe at all if you continue to punish him. Your job isn't to magnify his guilt or assuage it. Believe me, just seeing you every day will remind him of what he's done. If you embellish the guilt he's already carrying, you may get what you want in terms of some temporary slavish devotion, but ultimately you may well drive him away.

Allison: But am I just supposed to "drop it"? Doesn't he owe me?

Susan: Of course he owes you. But let's be real clear on what he owes you. He owes you honesty and respect. Let's go back to your list of requirements for a minute. These conditions for continuing in the relationship are very specific. Scott's agreed to a particular set of changes that are aimed at making reparations for the damage done by his lies, and he's promised to stop lying. But where are the demands that he give up his adult autonomy, his right to disagree with you, and most of all, his dignity? You want to be in a relationship of equals, not some kind of dictator-subject craziness.

If you find yourself doing a lot of guilt-tripping, it will help enormously to acknowledge that to him. Tell him that just as you've agreed to give him time to change, he needs to understand that you're not a saint and you're undoubtedly going to say, or already have said, things that make him feel awful. Don't worry about weakening your position with that kind of acknowledgment. You will actually be exhibiting a very special kind of strength—one that comes from self-awareness and truthfulness.

Punishing Behavior No. 2: Belittling and Denigrating

He's volunteered to work with your son's Boy Scout troop. "That's a joke!" you tell him. "A guy with no morals thinking he can be a role model for a bunch of impressionable kids. What planet are you from?"

Or maybe he wants to go sailing with his brother instead of visiting your parents with you. No surprise there, you tell him. He's the thoughtless, selfish pig who lost a lot of money in some harebrained investment, so of course he's putting himself first. In fact, anytime he wants something different, you remind him of how selfish he is.

This strategy makes his transgressions a description of his total character. He's so flawed, you let him know, that he's unqualified to do anything else but penance for the lies he's told. It's easy to lash out and make him the scapegoat for everything. How can he possibly atone? By meeting your every demand.

Everything you learned above about guilt-tripping applies here. It's destructive. Try to drop it.

Punishing Behavior No. 3: Withdrawal

When they're deeply hurt, many women withdraw into a punishing silence that can be every bit as loud as the strategies we've seen so far.

Helen, whose husband, Phil, had lied to her about cybersex, had come a long way in being able to control her name-calling and caustic criticism. But she had disconnected from Phil in the process and didn't know what to do next:

We've made some progress. I've agreed to stop lashing out at him, and he's agreed to significantly limit his time at the computer, and I guess I can live with that. At least he's not sneaking around in the middle of the night and lying about what he's doing. I don't feel furious anymore, but I don't feel love for him. I've just gone kind of numb.

Helen may have felt numb, but she had gone from expressing her rage at Phil in very overt but belittling ways to punishing him by withdrawing—a powerful form of emotional blackmail. They were determined to stay together, but their relationship had deteriorated to a polite freeze.

"Pass the salt" and "Nice day, isn't it?" is about the extent of our conversation right now. I don't know how to get past this, Susan. I know what I'm doing isn't working. It's certainly not making either one of us feel good, but I don't seem to be able to help myself. I'm afraid if I'm nicer to him he'll think he can go right back to his old behavior. . . .

I told both of them that the cold war needed to come to an end. They agreed, but expressed concern about how to thaw their frozen relationship. Phil was bewildered by Helen's continuing withdrawal when he had agreed to all her conditions. They were both noticeably tense at the beginning of the session.

I asked Helen if she would be willing to tell Phil why she was afraid to express any positive feelings toward him. She began tentatively:

I've been so angry and so hurt, and it's hard to turn all of that off and just be loving. I guess I'm still trying to punish you, but now I'm doing it with silence instead of words. . . . To be perfectly honest, what I'm realizing is that I'm punishing myself too. I don't like being so cold and distant—in fact I hate it. I'm just so afraid that you won't take me seriously if I loosen up.

Phil answered,

Hon, after that confrontation, you don't ever have to worry that I'm not taking you seriously. But how long are you going to keep this up—how are we ever going to have any happiness again if you won't meet me halfway? I'm doing everything you asked of me, and I've promised to stop lying to you—and I have. I know it's still early, but I liked it better when you were bawling me out. At least then there was some feeling. This way, I feel so . . .

At this point Phil began to tear up and his voice broke. Like many men, especially of his generation, he didn't express his feelings easily.

"You feel so what, Phil?" I asked him. "Tell Helen."

"Lonely. . . . It's worse than actually being alone because you're there but I can't reach you. . . ."

I turned to Helen, who was noticeably moved. "Tell Phil what's going on with you now."

Helen put her head down and said softly, "I'm sorry . . . I know I've been cold. I guess I was trying to make you suffer as much as I have. I can't guarantee that it will all be tied up with blue ribbons now, but at least we're talking to each other again, and that feels really good."

The logjam was broken, to everyone's relief. I told Helen that when she had said "that feels really good," she had just put into practice one of the most profound methods for moving away from punishing and into some real dialogue—giving feedback. And I hoped they would both do more of it when they were together.

Feedback as a Tool for Connecting

Feedback is a natural complement to the active listening you've already been doing. Effective feedback:

- Tells your partner what your reaction is
- Avoids judgment
- Is immediate, honest, and supportive

Good feedback sounds like this:

- "I like that."
- "That doesn't feel good to me."
- "I feel uncomfortable with that."
- "I feel included in that."
- "You sound enthusiastic/willing/sincere, and that makes me feel good."

I told Helen and Phil that as obvious as it sounds, we need to remember that nobody changes overnight. People often fall back on old patterns, especially under stress. But they had taken a big step toward the very human, and sometimes slow, process of learning to be different with each other. They both had a lot of old patterns to replace, and they needed to be patient and not beat up on each other or themselves if they weren't doing everything perfectly all the time.

Turning Off Sexually

"There's something else we need help with," Phil said, and I was pretty sure what was coming. "She's, uh, turned off to me in other ways too. . . ."

"And," added Helen, "it doesn't help to have you pressuring me. It would be such a relief if you'd just back off for a while. I'm still pretty shell-shocked, and I can't just jump into bed with you and pretend nothing happened."

"Gee," I said to Phil, "what a surprise. Your wife is mad at you and she doesn't feel sexy."

"Sexy, hell," said Phil, "she won't even let me put my arm around her. She scoots all the way over to the edge of her side of the bed, turns her back to me, and goes to sleep. How long is that going to go on?"

"I don't know," I answered, "but I can promise you one thing: the more you pressure, the longer it will take for her to feel sexual or even affectionate with you again. Many—maybe even most—women turn off sexually with their partners for a period of time after the discovery that they've been lied to. It's difficult for a woman to feel sexy when she's been deceived and is struggling with so many conflicting emotions."

I suggested to Helen and Phil that they do a little bartering. Each one would give the other something the other one wanted and agree not to do something that made the other one uncomfortable.

I asked Helen what she would be willing to give as her portion of the barter. She thought for a while and said, "I certainly would be willing to let Phil express some physical affection toward me. I mean we could start with hand-holding and, when it felt comfortable, progress to some hugging and kissing, but nothing more unless I wanted it. That would be fine as long as he doesn't take that as a sign—"

At that point I stopped her:

"Hold it, Helen. You just need to offer him something—let's not write the script about what he might or might not do."

I then asked Helen to tell Phil what she needed from him.

"I need time, and I need your patience. I know it's not easy for you when I've been so rejecting. I want my sexual feelings to come back as much as you do, and I honestly believe they will. But for right now, you need to let me initiate that when I'm ready."

Phil agreed to Helen's request as his part of the barter. A few weeks later, Helen told me that Phil was honoring the agreement and that just removing the sexual pressure created a space for her sexual feelings to return.

You Both Need to Give You Time

A lot of women have told me that after confrontation, their partner has taken the position "OK, I apologized, I heard you out, I agreed to all your conditions. Now let's go to bed and make love"—and then become upset when it didn't quite work out that way. Men often see sexual withdrawal as the ultimate punishment. A man may understand why his partner is turned off to him, especially if she's discovered he's been cheating on her, but he doesn't understand why she isn't able to respond to him immediately once he's admitted his lies and started working on his part in repairing the relationship.

If this is happening to you, you need to remind your lover that for you, as for most women, sexual feelings don't exist in limbo. They are deeply connected to feelings of safety and emotional closeness, both of which have been seriously impaired by his lying. You need to set up the same kind of barter that brought Helen and Phil closer together. You may want to say things like:

- "I know you're frustrated and hurt because I'm not feeling very sexual right now."
- "Please understand, I'm not doing this to punish you."
- "I have to be true to my own feelings, and right now I'm not feeling sexy."

- "I know this won't last and that things will get better with a little time."

If you had sexual feelings for him before you found out about his lies, chances are good they will come back once you feel less wounded. You've been stunned, and you have every right to ask for and expect to get some time to heal. Your erogenous zones are directly connected to your mind and your heart. When they are less traumatized, your sexual feelings will follow suit.

Holding Back Even When You Want to Make Love
Allison had a different dilemma:

I want to make love. I love sex with him, and as amazing as it may sound, I want him even after everything. But I won't let myself. I keep getting pictures in my mind of him and that woman that worked for him. I can hear him saying all the adorable, sexy things he's said to me, and I see him doing all the erotic things he did with me, and I think, the hell with him. Why should I reward him for what he did? Why shouldn't his behavior cost him something?

Allison was holding back even though she still had sexual feelings for Scott because she didn't think he'd suffered enough. In addition, she probably didn't want to give him the satisfaction of seeing she still wanted him. All this was certainly punishing Scott, but Allison was punishing herself as well—not only by depriving herself of sexual pleasure but by the endless replaying of painful fantasies.

The Movie in Your Mind
"OK," said Allison, "I admit I'm torturing myself with these pictures. I've got her looking like Sharon Stone and of course absolutely wild in bed . . . but how do I stop?"

If you're like Allison and your lover's lies were about other women, the obsessive, intrusive thoughts and pictures in your mind are probably running relentlessly. Not surprisingly, they're a major impediment to feeling sexual or loving. In fact, they're driving you crazy. Sometimes they're most vivid when you think about making love. It's as if there's a whole audiovisual system in your bedroom programmed to play only your most torturous thoughts and images. Let's turn the system off.

I know how difficult this can be, especially when the wounds are fresh. Obsessive thoughts seem to have a life all their own and invade your head like some marauding army. But there are some very effective exercises to help you start using your imagination to help rather than hurt yourself. As with all of our work together, it won't happen overnight, but you will get much better with practice.

Become a Movie Critic

The first thing I would like you to do is write a capsule review of your movie.

Allison had actually seen her husband, Scott, being romantic with another woman, so her movie was especially vivid. I asked her to imagine that she was a movie critic and was assigned to write a short review of what she'd seen and was continuing to see in her mind.

Here's what her review said:

"I hate this movie. In fact, I hate it more than any movie I've ever seen. I do not recommend this movie to anybody! It's so bad it shouldn't even go right to video—it should go right to the trash bin. The plot sucks and the acting sucks. On a scale of one to ten it's a minus ten. I give it thumbs down, no stars or checks."

Write a review of the movie in *your* mind. Don't censor yourself. Make your review really scathing, and use humor as much as possible. Really put this movie down in no uncertain terms. This is the beginning of disempowering the images that are invading your head.

Put Yourself in the Director's Chair

I'm a great believer in symbols and rituals. I like their immediacy and the fact that they give us something tangible and familiar to work with. Most important, symbols and rituals are astoundingly effective at reprogramming the unconscious and diminishing disturbing thoughts and feelings.

Next, I'm going to ask you to work with an object that is

familiar to all of us—your TV or VCR remote control. I want you to use any remote in your house that you can carry around with you without inconveniencing yourself when you want to watch something. If you don't have a remote that you're not using, buy one. I promise you it will be worth the trouble.

The remote control symbolizes just that—control. For the next couple of weeks, keep the remote with you—in your purse, your desk drawer, next to your favorite chair, or in the glove compartment of your car. Pull it out whenever you're invaded by the unwanted images, and push the off button, just as you would if you were turning off your set. Now, let that imagination of yours take over. See the hurtful images, press the off button, watch as the images fade to black. Continue to see that black screen for at least thirty seconds. For those thirty seconds you are in total control. Practice creating the movie, watching your husband with another woman you conjure up, tolerate the pain for a few moments, and then *turn it off!*

Decrease the time you watch the movie and increase the time the screen is black each day. This exercise puts you in the director's chair. You can call "Action" or "Cut" when you want to. Soon you'll find that you can go to black whenever you want or need to. After all, it's your movie.

The Movie Vault

Another option we all have if we're watching something we don't like on television is to switch to something else instead of turning the set off.

I know it's hard to believe when the images (or horror movies, as I prefer to call them) seem to have a life of their own. I know you don't consciously decide "OK, it's four in the morning and I feel like suffering, so I'll just lie here and picture my lover with another woman." Few of us are that masochistic. I also know how helpless you feel to stop. While you're in the throes of these fantasies, it's easy to forget that no one can put those pictures there but you. The good news is that you can also change them. Your mind is a wondrous device. Now you're going to transform that mental energy into some positive rather than painful images. You need to watch a different program.

In the warehouse of your mind, thousands of movies are stored. They are your memories as well as your happier fantasies. In this warehouse are comedies as well as tragedies, adventure movies, movies about children and animals, and travelogues of beautiful places. You'll notice I didn't mention love stories—I don't think those are the best kinds of movies for you to watch right now.

When the horror movie comes into your mind, push the channel changer button on your remote and switch to another program. Now start to see something that makes you feel good. That something can be images of a beautiful place you've been, a happy family occasion or outing—you know where you need to go in order to evoke pleasurable feelings.

For me, that picture is a bay on the island of Hawaii that is one of the most beautiful spots on earth. When I put myself there, I can see the sun sparkling on the water and the green-black mountains. I can feel the soft air and smell the perfume of the flowers. I can hear the surf and the chirping of birds. All of my senses are stimulated. I'm with people I love, and I feel their presence strongly. I feel happy and at peace. I go there in my mind whenever I feel stressed out or upset, and within a few moments I feel calmer. There is no room in my special place for negative thoughts or painful memories or images.

You have had experiences like that. You have a place like that. See yourself there. Feel everything about it—drink it in. Immerse your senses in the experience. That's the movie you want to watch—not the one you've been watching. The more you can consciously choose to replace the horror movie with one that gives you pleasure, the sooner you will be able to drive the bad movie out of your mind.

I know that at first glance these exercises may seem simplistic to you, and you may be skeptical about their effectiveness. I can assure you that over the years they have proven to have a profound impact on women's ability to take charge of their painful thoughts and feelings instead of being at their mercy. Try them—you'll like them. You might even find yourself making love again. What have you got to lose?

PUNISHING BEHAVIOR NO. 4: THREATS

The other side of quiet, angry withdrawal is the much more overt strategy of holding the threat of ending the relationship over his head. "Do it my way or you're out of here" is the name of this self-defeating game. After all, you think, you're the victim and he's on probation.

This emotional arm-twisting plays on his very natural fears that you'll leave him if he doesn't do everything exactly to your specifications. This type of threat typically sounds like this:

- "Go ahead, do what you want, but don't be surprised if I'm not around for long."
- "If you're going to disagree with me so much, why should I stay with you after what you did to me?"
- "Do things my way, or I'll make sure your family knows everything you did to me."

This strategy is a distinctive way of continually reminding him of his lies and how much he's in your debt because you've agreed to stay. If he has needs or opinions of his own, that's tantamount to another betrayal. You'd be surprised how many otherwise reasonable, caring women fall into this behavior.

If you find yourself engaging in this form of emotional blackmail (give me my way or else), it's a good idea to remind your partner that you're both going to make mistakes during this difficult period. You might want to say something like:

"This is a tough time for both of us. We both have to realize things aren't going to get magically better overnight. I know you're doing your best and I need to stop threatening you."

Punishing him won't bring back the good feelings that it hurt so much to lose. More than anything else, you need time to figure out if it's possible to reconnect with the warmth and desire you once had for your lover. If that's not your goal, and just getting back at him is the real reason you've decided to stay with him, you're both going to be miserable.

In the aftermath of confrontation, I know it's easy to fall into a cycle of punishment. But as corny as it may sound, none of that will undo the past or make you feel any better. Remember, the fabric of everyday life gets worn very thin by this kind of pushing and pulling. You may get a lot of momentary satisfaction out of rubbing his nose in his bad behavior, but you risk losing a relationship that might very well evolve into something good.

HANDLING PRESSURE FROM FAMILY AND FRIENDS

The emotional exhaustion you are probably feeling at this point may be intensified by the well-meaning advice of other people in your life. Those who've seen you crying or angry may believe that the best thing for you is to get out of the relationship. Conversely, others may pressure you to make a commitment to stay no matter what.

Whichever stance they take, the important thing in dealing with people outside the relationship is to set very firm boundaries about how much you're willing to talk with them about what's going on and where you draw the line.

Family members and friends have their own subjective perceptions and often their own agendas and may, without realizing it, try to push us one way or the other because it's in their best interests to do so—but it's not always in ours. Certainly we all need confidants, and most of us have one or several people in our lives we open up to completely. But it's important that you let everyone know you're not going to be pressured into any kind of decision beyond the one you've already made.

For now, I'm going to show you some ways to deal with the people who are pressuring you to leave despite the fact that you have decided to see whether you and your partner can make a fresh start. In the next chapter, we'll take a look at how to handle pressure from people who are urging you to stay in a hopeless situation. Friends or family may say things like:

- "I can't stand to see what he's doing to you—you've got to get out now."
- "Why are you kidding yourself? He'll never change."
- "How can you stay with him after all he's done to you?"
- "How many more times are you going to let him hurt you?"
- "You're too good for him."

- "He doesn't deserve you."
- "I knew he was a bastard from the minute I met him."
- "You'd better get out now—you're not getting any younger."

Your job in the face of these sometimes well-meaning, sometimes self-serving attempts to influence you is to learn a series of responses that will allow you to hold your ground without coming across as belligerent. If you argue, explain, try to justify your position, try to get them to see your point of view, or get angry, you will immediately be putting yourself on the defensive. You'll feel one-down and frustrated, with your back against the wall. It's far better and more empowering to answer their comments with gentle but forceful comments like:

- "I appreciate your concern, but this is really between my husband and me."
- "I know you really care about me, but I have to find my own way with this."
- "I love you and know you mean well, but I'm much stronger now and I know I will make a thoughtful and healthy decision."
- "Could you just hear me out without giving any advice?"
- "We're both working very hard to rebuild our relationship. I'm sorry if you have a problem with that. I hope you'll respect whatever decision I make."
- "I'm not willing to walk away without giving him one more chance. If he screws up again, believe me, I won't stay with him."

Anne told me that her mother was beside herself when Anne told her what had happened with Randy:

I've used most of those statements with her, and she backs off for a while, but then she starts up again. "How can you know he won't do it again? You can't watch him twenty-four hours a day." I know she loves me, but she's tapping right into my own fears. I don't want to be rude or mean with her, but I've got to find a way to put a stop to this.

If someone you're close to continues to barrage you with
what they think you should do and fails to back off after you have
used some of these responses, you have every right to say:

- "You know what—I'm not willing to talk about this
  anymore."
- "Let's change the subject. Have you seen any good
  movies lately?"
- "Enough!"

Don't ever forget, family and friends have a right to their
opinion, but you have a right not to have to listen to it. Women
often fall into the trap of thinking they have to listen to everything, hear everyone out, answer every question, all in the service
of being a "nice person." There is nothing mean or not nice in setting limits on how much you're willing to listen to someone else's
ideas about what's best for you. Especially if you didn't ask for
them in the first place!

HOW ARE YOU DOING?

As time passes, you'll be able to see and sense the change in your
relationship. You'll have a better idea of whether the two of you,
as a couple, can move beyond the damage done by the lying and
have a future together. The healing process, even under the best
circumstances, can be tentative and slow. You'll need to be
patient and know that getting discouraged is normal.

Every few days at first, and then every week, I'd like you to
set aside some time to check in with yourself and take stock of
how you're doing. Ask yourself:

- What is feeling good about the relationship and what still
  needs to change?
- What gives me hope?
- What do I worry about?
- What makes me feel discouraged?
- Has he stopped abusing alcohol/drugs?
- Is he staying within the financial boundaries we agreed on?

- Am I fulfilling my part of the agreement and using constructive communication instead of constantly punishing him?
- Are we both making use of outside resources to help us, when indicated?

These questions will guide you in the weeks ahead. They will give you a framework for exploring your thoughts, feelings, and behavior. They will also serve as signposts for the ongoing evaluation you will need to make about your own well-being and your partner's behavior, as well as your relationship. You might want to share some of your answers with him as a way of expressing both appreciation and concern.

I urge you to keep a journal of your answers to these questions and to compare your first set of answers with the ones you give as you progress. Your journal will serve as a tangible record of your progress.

NO GUARANTEES

When betrayal, especially sexual betrayal, is a known quantity, overcoming jealousy and suspicion is a real challenge. One question constantly nags at you: How can you be sure he won't betray you again?

The answer is probably not what you want to hear. You can't. There are no guarantees. Betrayal is always a possibility in any relationship. So what's the point of obsessing about it? The one thing I can guarantee is that if you wall yourself off and become hypervigilant, constantly searching for the next lie, you'll never give your relationship a chance to right itself.

The devastating power of jealousy is in its ability to create compelling dramas from the stuff of everyday life. Seen through the lens of jealousy, a glance is never just a glance, and a casually scribbled phone number on a notepad is a sure sign of conspiracy. It's easy to be pulled in by the complex scenarios that suspicion creates.

Jealousy and suspicion will eat away at your soul, and they're powerful enough to rip the scabs off a newly mended relationship and keep the wounds fresh, unable to heal. None of this is meant to encourage you to slide into total gullibility. I would never suggest that you substitute blind trust for staying tuned in to your senses and your intuition. But as you move into a new phase of your relationship, uncertain of what to expect or believe, you must actively work each day to keep suspicion and jealousy from becoming the forces that hold you back from any chance of rediscovering intimacy. The exercises you saw above for stopping and changing the movies in your mind can be very helpful in ending an obsessive cycle of jealousy. I encourage you to be aware of the repetitive thoughts that give rise to suspicion and to work actively to change them. Doing that, and paying attention to real changes in your lover's behavior, will give you the best chance for rebuilding.

THE CHALLENGE OF CHANGE

Change creates a sense of uncertainty for everyone. No matter how unhappy some parts of your relationship were, there was a certain predictability before, but now, nothing is predictable. It's natural for one or both of you to yearn to "just go back to the way we were" and leap over all the pain and hard work. But the way you were was a facade. There was a lot of illusion and a lot of secrecy. Now the dark side of your relationship has come to the surface, and you have to come to terms with it. Things are changing internally and externally, and there's no magic date by which all the tension will disappear, but if you and your lover both do your part, little by little it will.

11

If You Leave

Some relationships can survive even after they've been torn by lies. Others won't. There's no easy formula for adding up the pros and cons and saying "It's time." There's rarely one reason or a specific timetable. There is simply that moment, after weeks or months of putting care and energy into rebuilding what you had together, when a sure, quiet voice inside you says, "It's over."

It may be that you've discovered that he's lied to you yet again and that the commitments he's made to you have been all but forgotten. Or you may find as you start focusing much more actively on what you want that this relationship cannot give it to you. Or it may be that you wake up one morning and know with finality that you can never regain even a semblance of what you once had. Sometimes, even if both of you are trying hard, you've reached the point of no return. You just don't love him anymore.

"MY LOVE JUST DIED"

I was sad but not surprised to learn from Jan that she had discovered there was far more to Bill's neglecting to tell her about a former wife than she originally realized. We had both been delighted with Bill's unequivocal commitment to stop withholding important information from Jan, regardless of how it might make him look in her eyes. But I was always skeptical about the notorious "picture in the glove compartment" story and what Bill's bizarre explanation really indicated about what was truth and what was fiction.

I had not seen Jan for almost a year after the brief crisis work we did together, but one day she called and asked me to see her as soon as I could. She was red-eyed and distraught when she came in:

It's over! I've really been played for a fool! I can't believe what's been going on—I'm still in a state of shock. The other night after dinner the phone rang and Bill answered it. I heard him saying "Just a minute—let me take this in the other room." I heard him go into the bedroom and close the door. I know I shouldn't have, Susan, but something inside me got very scared, so very carefully I picked up the extension so it didn't make a click—

"Oh, god," I said, "I think that's the way over half the women in the world find out about their partner's affair. So who was it—the ex-wife whose picture you found in the car or somebody else?"

Ex-wife number two. The one whose picture I found in the glove compartment. He's been seeing her all along! I heard my husband, who's always telling me how much he loves me and that I'm the best thing that ever happened to him and he can't wait to get home from the office and all that bullshit, saying to another woman that he's got to find a way for them to be together more often. Then she asks if he can come over for a while, and he says, "Sure—I'll just tell Jan I've got to take some papers over to a client."
When he came out of the bedroom, he took one look at my face and he knew. He tried to tell me another cock-and-bull story. If this had been some one-night stand, maybe I could have dealt with it. But this wasn't just sex—he's never fully disconnected from her—he admits that. So he not only betrayed me sexually, he betrayed me emotionally, which is a lot worse. When I looked at him at that moment, I saw a stranger. All the lies, all the stories—my love just died. I've been crying nonstop, but I'm very clear on what I need to do.

Jan had indeed reached the point of no return. She had some heavy-duty grieving ahead of her, and her resolve might waver from time to time, but she had made her decision based on clear evidence that Bill was a man she could neither trust nor believe in again. With that realization, she knew that her love was gone.

AM I DOING THE RIGHT THING?

For some women, making the decision to end an important relationship can be more painful and draining than the actual ending. You can expect to be assailed by doubts and regrets. Paralyzing fear seems to jump out at you from every corner. You're in uncharted territory, and you're probably exhausting yourself with second-guessing.

Diane and Ben were one couple I thought had a chance to make it, but unfortunately, Ben's financial recklessness and need to make the "big deal" were more powerful than the commitments he made to Diane.

Ben had agreed to involve her much more actively in financial decisions. They were able to avoid bankruptcy with the help of a financial counselor and a loan from Diane's mother. But it wasn't long before Ben's old demons started acting up again:

Things were fairly stable for a while. We had a budget worked out; he was doing what the financial counselor was suggesting. We've basically been living on my salary, and he promised to look for something in the real estate field that would be steady. I agreed to keeping both names on our accounts because I didn't want to totally emasculate him when he's had such a rotten time of it. Besides, I don't want to live with a man I have to treat like a child. But he is a child, Susan. An irresponsible, deceptive child.

You know the fifty thousand dollars my mother lent us to pay off our creditors? Well, I made the mistake of leaving some of it in the bank, and guess what? A friend of his came to him with a "sure thing"—they both had to put in ten thousand dollars within two days to buy some land in foreclosure. I went ballistic when he told me about it and said, "No way—that money's all earmarked for obligations we've incurred." He got very quiet and said I was right. Yesterday I got the bank statement. He'd withdrawn the money by cashier's check. He'll never change. Not even

the threat of losing me is enough to stop him. He's like an addict.
But how can I be sure I've made the right decision?

To help give Diane a snapshot of the relationship as it existed right now, I asked her to answer some important questions. I urge you to do the same. This is a valuable checklist to help guide you through the valley of decision.

- Have I given myself enough time to evaluate how he's responding to my conditions?
- Is he meeting the conditions he agreed to when I confronted him?
- Am I acting on pure impulse and emotion rather than reason and logic?
- Am I ending the relationship just to punish him?
- Is the relationship enriching, expanding, and fulfilling me? Or is it continuing to depress me, scare me, anger me, and narrow my life?

Diane answered yes to the first question and a strong no to the second, third, and fourth. When she came to the last question she became visibly sad:

I'd have to say it's definitely narrowing my life. There's no joy left, no trust. And worst of all, I've lost all respect for him. I used to find his energy and his grandiosity exciting, but now they just scare me. He scares me so much it makes me sick. I've got to get off this roller coaster and get some sanity back in my life.

As you look more critically at your partner the way Diane was doing, you may see him differently from the way you did before. And in this new light, sometimes something shifts inside. It becomes impossible to gloss over the negative, chaotic aspects of your life together or to deny your true feelings.

DEALING WITH HIS RESPONSE TO YOUR DECISION

There's no way to predict how your lover will respond when he realizes what his lying has cost him. Once you've let him know of your decision to end the relationship, you need to be prepared to handle a wide spectrum of reactions, some of which may surprise you. He's going to feel frightened and threatened. A very aggressive man may become pathetic and pleading. A passive or subdued man may become belligerent. His defenses are down, and your decision is clearly not what he wants, or even believed could happen. That's why I want to help you prepare yourself for whatever he says and does.

BRAVE WORDS

You may feel shaky or frightened or overwhelmed with pity for him in the face of his response to you, but using brave words will help you hold fast. Even if you don't feel brave, it's important to act as if you do. I promise you, your feelings will catch up.

He's quite likely to say things like:

- "I don't know how you can do this to me."
- "Please give me another chance—I'll never lie to you again."
- "I've been doing the best I can. Please give me more time."
- "I know you still love me—somebody's just put these crazy ideas into your head."
- "You're making a mistake you'll regret for the rest of your life."
- "You'll never find anyone to love you as much as I do."
- "The kids need a father—have you thought of them at all?"
- "You never think of anyone but yourself."

Listen to him, and as you do, tell yourself three things:

1. I believe in myself and my decision.
2. I am acting to create a better life for myself.
3. He will survive, and so will I.

Then answer him with any or all of the following brave words, and any other appropriate ones you come up with on your own:

- "I didn't come to this decision lightly. I've given it a great deal of thought and my decision is firm."
- "It's really hard for me to see you hurting like this, but this is not negotiable."
- "I'm very sad/angry/frightened/upset too. But this is what I need to do."
- "I've worked hard to see the solutions open to me, and this is the one I've chosen."

ERR ON THE SIDE OF CAUTION

When Bill saw that Jan was not going to be swayed by promises or pleading, he turned nasty:

"He was tight-lipped and his eyebrows drew together in that scowl I've seen whenever he's thwarted. When I told him I wanted him out by morning, he got up from the couch, picked up a book I'd been reading, and slammed it into the wall. Then he went into the bedroom and slammed the door so hard the whole house shook. He's never aimed his anger at me in any physical way, and this was really scary. I called my sister and told her the kids and I needed to stay with her for a few days. I got the kids out of school, and left. I figured I'd better play it safe."

Chances are that the wall was the only thing Bill was going to hit, but even if there was one chance in a hundred that he might go further, it was wise of Jan not to take the risk. If your partner becomes angry and at all threatening, don't worry about your communication skills—think of your safety first. Even a man who has never acted out his anger in a physical way may become explosive when confronted with the reality that it's really over.

Now it's time to deal with *your* reactions to your decision.

THE TWIN DEMONS OF GUILT AND SELF-REPROACH

No matter how painful the lies and the life they created for you, it's never easy to witness the pain that arises at an ending that was not what both people wanted. The tears, anger, bewilderment, and disbelief of someone you have loved and probably still care for are not easy to withstand. You may find your resolve weakening at the sight of how pathetic he looks. You may find yourself very tempted to back down and give him that one more chance, rationalizing with thoughts like "Better the devil you know than the devil you don't know" or "I've got so much time and emotion invested in him, maybe it's better to tough it out and hope for the best."

The understandable ambivalence many women feel at this time gives birth to a set of evil twins: guilt and self-reproach. When this pair takes over, you may find yourself starting to believe that it's you, not he, who's responsible for the death of the relationship.

THE BURDEN OF UNDESERVED GUILT

He's lied, he's betrayed you, he's deceived you, he's broken his promises to you, but you're the one who's feeling guilty. And he may be doing all in his power to let you know how your decision to leave is making him suffer or even destroying him.

Diane had to deal with just such guilt when she filed for divorce:

Even though I hate what he's done, it's really hard to see him so devastated. He used to be so alive and full of optimism. He's staying with an old college chum and his wife because he doesn't even have enough for a motel. But at least I know he has a decent place to stay. He keeps calling and saying, "I can't believe you would leave me because of ten thousand dollars." He really believes this is just about money. I get these terrible waves of guilt, like I'm somehow the bad guy here, and then I start the "Maybe he can change" or "Maybe I'm overreacting."

I told Diane that she was rewriting history in an attempt to assuage her guilt for having made the man she once loved so miserable. She knew how dependent Ben had become on her, both emotionally and financially, and she knew how much her decision was hurting him. But she also knew there was no magic pill that would turn Ben into the stable, responsible man she had hoped he would be. I asked her if any of Ben's promises or commitments resulted in sustained, positive behavioral change. I think you know her answer.

If you've been shoring up a man whose lies have gotten him

into trouble in other parts of his life, you may feel guilty that you won't be there to bail him out. Or you may have a belief system that says it's "selfish" to look out for yourself in the face of his pain over your decision. You may believe you "owe" him for the good things he's done for you. And you may feel enormous guilt because you are, to use a tired phrase, "breaking up the family."

For centuries, women have been the appointed guardians of relationships. It has traditionally been up to us to be the nurturers, the caregivers, the fixers. If the relationship is troubled, it's been our job to put it right, no matter what. These mandates are deeply ingrained in women of every age, no matter how hip or liberated they may be.

If you've done your share of the work and have made the decision that your relationship is over, don't add to the stress and hurt you're struggling with by loading yourself down with undeserved guilt. Take responsibility for the negative, cruel, nasty, or unhealthy things you've said and done. Acknowledge them (even to him, if you think it's appropriate), and tolerate your guilt as you do what you need to do. Guilt diminishes over time. The impact on your well-being if you stay locked in a relationship ruined by lying does not. You have a new mandate: to have as rich and fulfilling a life as you can make for yourself. Those are not goals for everybody else in the world but you, and they're not the stuff fairy tales are made of. They are your basic human rights. Remind yourself of that whenever you find your guilt is working overtime to make you forget the reasons you need to leave.

You're Not a Failure

Even Carol, who had tolerated years of her husband's alcoholism and abuse, was beset with self-reproach when she finally made her decision to divorce him after he lied about having left their son alone on a camping trip:

If anybody has a right to get a divorce, it's me, right? So why am I feeling so lousy about myself? Why do I still cling to the belief that there was something more I could have done? Why do I feel like such a failure?

"Carol," I answered, "you've been the glue that's held this relationship together. You've done everything humanly possible, and Ken hasn't done a damn thing except exactly what he wants, with no concern about you or your feelings. He won't do anything about his drinking, he's emotionally abusive, and you've had signs that he can become physically violent at any time. You've given him every chance, but things have only gotten worse. Please don't condemn yourself as weak or a failure because his lies and his behavior have caused damage that can't be repaired. Yes, you took a vow to stay together until 'death do us part.' But it was Ken who changed the terms of the marriage contract, not you. There is nothing sacred about a marriage that has been torn apart by lying and betrayal."

Carol's only "failure" was her decision to stay in an unhappy, destructive relationship for as long as she did. Her strict religious upbringing, combined with her shame about being the first one in her family to get a divorce, kept her there much longer than was good for either her or her children. It's actually a great success—indeed, a triumph—when a woman finds the strength to say, "Enough! I deserve better."

IN THE CHILDREN'S BEST INTERESTS

It's almost a given that you will feel guilt and self-reproach knowing that you will be putting your children through some unhappy times.

But ask yourself, who is more likely to provide the kind of environment in which children can flourish—a stressed-out, unhappy set of parents who no longer have a relationship based on trust and mutual respect, or a woman living with integrity on her own? Children learn from what they see and hear more than from whatever you may tell them in an effort to minimize the tension between your partner and you. If what they see is bitterness and mistrust, you'll be infusing them with the message that this is what relationships are supposed to be like. You will be showing them a model of marriage in which men can lie and get away with it, and women are supposed to accept whatever they get.

Remember the story of Carol and her daughter, Paula, whom I saw many years later? Paula gravitated toward a man who was totally insensitive about her rape experience and lied when it suited his purposes:

In many ways, I think I reenacted in my life what was going on when I was a child. It was what I was familiar with. I thought that's the way love was supposed to feel. I never learned anything else. It was so different after my mother and father split up. So much calmer and saner for my brother and me. I saw her change, so I know that can happen.

In a few short sentences, Paula summed up the legacy of her childhood. She insightfully realized how much impact her mother and father's relationship had had in shaping her ideas and perceptions about relationships. Her parents stayed together until Paula was fifteen, and I have a strong belief that Paula would have chosen a better partner for herself had she not been exposed to the unhealthy relationship between her mother and father for so many years.

I'm well aware, both personally and professionally, of the difficulties a divorce can create for children. But if you are truthful with them and allow them to talk out their feelings and fears while assuring them that they have done nothing to cause the breakup, you will all get through it. Children are amazingly resilient and can handle a lot as long as their feelings and self-worth are validated.

DOOMSDAY SCENARIOS

Perhaps the most difficult aspect of making a decision to leave is the fear that overtakes us. Our fears often seem like a massive knotted tangle of different-colored yarns—impossible to sort out. But you can unravel the thoughts and feelings that are panicking you and make them manageable.

Diane didn't look back after she made her final decision to leave Ben, but in looking ahead, she became frightened by how black the future looked to her:

I know I'm doing what's best for me. But then I start projecting into the future, and all I see is loneliness and depression. What if I'm alone for the rest of my life? What if I lose my job? What if I can't make it?

Diane was smart, attractive, and had good job skills as well as a lot of experience. She had kept the family afloat while Ben went through their money trying to make the big score. Yet she was overtaken by what I call doomsday scenarios—those bleak, larger-than-life catastrophic predictions that are familiar to most of you. Doomsday scenarios have no respect for the truth. They are lies we tell ourselves about the future. And the more we allow them to hold our attention, the faster they multiply. You can recognize them because they describe your life in horrendous absolutes, with words like *never, always, I can't, the rest of my life, forever.* If you're trapped in doomsday thinking, you're expressing your fears this way:

- I can't make it alone.
- I'll never find anyone else.
- I'll die of loneliness.
- I'll wind up a bag lady because I won't be able to support myself.
- I'm too old/too fat/too plain/too damaged for anyone to ever want me again.
- I'll never get over the pain.
- I don't know how to make new friends.

As thoughts like this crowd in, it becomes difficult to distinguish the real practical problems of separating from your partner and building a new life from the nightmarish exaggerations that doomsday scenarios evoke.

CHANGING CATASTROPHE TO REASONABLE CONCERN

Ending any relationship presents challenges, both practical and emotional. You may have to reorder your finances, change your social life, deal with the reactions of other people. And as if that weren't enough, if you have children you have to reach deep into yourself to find the strength to help them through this difficult time. Most important, you have to find the will and energy to take good care of yourself. These are reasonable concerns. And yes, it's very tough to handle all these things at once. But obsessive worrying about what's ahead will not solve anything and will only ensure that you are too emotionally exhausted to think straight.

It will be enormously comforting for you if you learn to make realistic plans for the future by transforming doomsday scenarios into reasonable concerns. I asked Diane to watch closely what happened to her panic level when we rephrased and restated her most dominant fears.

I suggested to Diane that she repeat her first statement, "All I see is loneliness and depression." Then I asked her to replace that scenario with "I'm concerned that there will be times when I'm lonely and depressed." That's a reasonable concern, and to it she could add a statement that began "But what I can do about that is . . ." That would help her open the door to thinking about realistic ways to combat what she feared.

Diane did just that. "What I can do about that is . . . see more of the friends I have and make some new ones. You know, I love to sing, and I've kind of let it go. Maybe I could get into a choir somewhere. I know I've got some very rough times ahead of me, but it feels lighter already just to shift my attention away from all the blackness and focus on some problem-solving."

I asked Diane to make a list of her most recurrent catastrophic fantasies—her doomsday scenarios—and do the same thing with all of them. Here's what her list looked like:

Catastrophic Thinking	Reasonable Concerns	Possible Solutions
I'll never find another lover.	Nobody can predict what may happen, but the chances are good I'll meet someone. It may take some time, but I have a lot of work to do on myself while I'm waiting.	Get into activities I enjoy. Spend time with friends. Let people know I'm available. Enjoy life free of lies. Rebuild my confidence.
I'll never find anyone as exciting as he is again.	I hope I can be attracted to someone stable and find him exciting.	Keep reminding myself how scary it was to live on the edge. I can go ride a roller coaster if I need that kind of excitement.

Catastrophic Thinking	Reasonable Concerns	Possible Solutions
I'll never be able to put my life back together.	I'm concerned about all the changes I have to make and all the things I need to do. It won't be easy, but I'll manage.	I can ask for help. I can put my concerns down on paper and take them one at a time. I can ask other people for advice and referrals. I can take classes to learn new skills.
I'm doomed to keep winding up with liars.	I'm concerned about why I stayed in the relationship so long, and I recognize how some of my behavior allowed a lot of the lying to continue.	I will keep working on my guilt and fears. I will keep using my new communication skills. I will keep my eyes and ears open, as well as my heart. I will not be afraid to confront lies if they occur.
If I don't go back to him, it will destroy him.	I'm concerned about his well-being but I have a responsibility to myself. He is the only one who can make his life better.	Be gentle but firm if he pressures me. Encourage him to get professional help if he is depressed. Enlist the help and support of his family and friends.

It's smart and realistic to say, "It might be tough, but . . ." or "I'm concerned about _____ but I'll manage." Doomsday scenarios that start with phrases like "I'll never" or "I can't" close off the part of your mind that wants to help you marshal your resources and find your way. "I can't" means "There's nothing I can do. I give up." Those are the thoughts that generate panic. They leave us completely vulnerable to the whims of fate because we've announced we have no control over our lives.

Whenever you start to feel overwhelmed by fears and worry, go back to your list. Add to the list of solutions as time goes by and you feel more energized and inventive. Remember, you're not alone. Millions of women have made it through situations like yours. Whatever comes up, you'll handle it.

SAYING GOOD-BYE TO YOUR RELATIONSHIP

No matter how ugly the betrayal, it does not mitigate the pain of having to leave behind a part of your life. In some instances it may have been a brief part and in others a major part, but the end of any relationship, even a bad one, is, as I've said before, a death. When a person dies, there are rituals to help us grieve and mark the magnitude of what has been lost. But the death of a relationship can leave us feeling adrift and filled with so much grief that we wonder if we'll ever be whole again.

Jan thought she was home free because she was so furious with Bill that there was little room for other feelings. But she was just delaying the inevitable:

I didn't expect to feel so torn up. I really hate him right now, but I have these enormous waves of sadness when I hear a certain song on the car radio or I start remembering what it was like when I had so much hope, so much love. I feel so awful for those two people who could have had so much and lost it. I feel like a part of me has died.

What was true for Jan will be true for you as well. Despite the lies, despite the betrayals, there were loving, joyful times and many periods of closeness. You can be grateful for those times, you can acknowledge that you miss them terribly, and you need to accept that they are gone. You need to have a ceremony for the ending just as you had a ceremony for the beginning. You need to write a eulogy to help you say good-bye to your relationship. This painful but essential step can help move you through your grieving.

PREPARING A EULOGY

There are four elements to your eulogy. Begin with the phrase "I hereby lay to rest the relationship of [your name] and [his name]." As with the eulogies you've heard at funerals, honor the good parts of the relationship. Then talk about the sadness and disappointment when lies and deception killed the relationship. End your eulogy with the familiar phrase that will signal the beginning of true healing for you: "Rest in peace."

Here's what Jan's eulogy looked like:

> I hereby lay to rest the marriage of Jan and Bill. It was a bright and shining thing—at the beginning. It was romantic and fun, and there was a lot of laughter. There were times of such intense happiness that it almost seemed as if they had cornered the market. But the brightness tarnished because there was betrayal and there were lies. And Bill was not the person he pretended to be. He was not good or honest or trustworthy. And so, the laughter turned to shock and disillusion, and the marriage became sick and finally died. Now it is time to put it to rest and to bury the good with the bad. We will grieve, but we will go on. Rest in peace.

Over the years, I have consistently found that writing something as heartfelt as a eulogy, while effective and healing, is only half as effective as reading it aloud. If you, like Jan, are in some form of counseling or support group, that is the ideal setting in which to read your eulogy. If not, you certainly can do it by yourself, or better yet, with someone you really trust with your most intimate emotions. But however you decide to do it, welcome the powerful emotions that this exercise will engender. Please don't hold them back. You will feel stronger after you've read it. There will be a sense of completion for you and a glimmer of hope for better times to come.

Although it may be hard to believe when you're swimming in the middle of it, little by little, step by step, grief does come to an end. You will not feel this way forever.

"CAN'T YOU GIVE HIM ONE MORE CHANCE?"

The people who care about you may act very differently from the friends and relatives of the woman who has decided to give her relationship another chance. Instead of urging you to leave, they may urge you to stay, put a lot of pressure on you, and do a lot of guilt-peddling as well.

Bill's widowed mother was devastated by Jan's decision to

leave her son, as was the rest of Bill's family. They were all, of course, unaware of the extent of Bill's deception. They thought Jan had never gotten over finding out he'd been married twice instead of once:

His mother called me and said, "Please give him another chance—you know he's really a good man, and you know how much we all love you. The other two never gave him the love and affection he needs, but he told me how wonderful you are and how much you mean to him. We really thought you were a gift from God. Everybody has problems. Surely you can work them out. After all, you've only been together four years—that's not enough time. We love having you as part of the family, and we love your children." Then she started crying. God, Susan, she's eighty years old. Should I tell her what he's done to me?

I told Jan that telling other people the real reasons for your decision to leave is a personal choice you can make after you've examined all the pros and cons. But whether you decide to tell all or not, you don't need to justify your decision to leave to any-one—and you don't need anyone else's approval to do what's best for you!

Chances are you've already taken several people into your confidence. Many of your friends, as well as whatever family members you are close to, may already have a pretty clear picture of what's been going on. You may want to be less specific with his family and friends. If you don't want to go into all the details, you can simply say:

- "I know how upsetting this is to you, but you don't know the full extent of what's been going on."
- "I didn't make this decision impulsively."
- "I want you to know that certain events have made it impossible for me to stay in this relationship."
- "I really appreciate how warm and caring you've been to me, and I hope that will continue."
- "You might want to ask your son/brother/buddy why I'm leaving him."

Although most of the pressure will probably come from his side of the aisle, you may be surprised by how upset some of the people in your family become when faced with the upheaval that the end to a relationship creates. They may fear being overwhelmed by your emotional needs. They may be apprehensive about dealing with you as a single woman. You may get bombarded by implications that you're not thinking of the children and reminders of the sanctity of marriage. Others may drag in that sturdy ally, religion, to pressure you into staying in an unhappy relationship and to cause you to start doubting your judgment.

As in any conflict, don't explain or give "good reasons." Where is it written that you have less right to decide the course of your life than they do? Hold to your nondefensive responses and remind the people close to you that what you need now is compassion and support, not a lecture.

LEAVING SOCIOPATHS—AND OTHER VOLATILE MEN

Dealing with a sociopath raises issues that may be similar to those that arise if the man you're leaving involved you in a relationship filled with drama, volatility, and emotional abuse. Though this section is intended primarily for women in relationships with sociopaths, please be aware that if you were with a man whose highs and lows resembled those of Jekyll and Hyde, much of what I say here will apply to you. Being with a man like this subjects you to a lot of excitement along with the distress and can create tight bonds between the two of you. Even if the word *sociopath* does not apply in your situation, the emotions, especially the self-reproach that accompanies ending a long relationship with such a man, may sound very familiar. I hope you'll read carefully and use whatever feels helpful.

If you have recognized that you're involved with a sociopath, your first order of business is to get him out of your life as quickly as possible. It's important to stay focused on the practical issues until he's gone, because his presence will impede and sabotage any attempt at healing.

I would be less than candid if I told you it was going to be easy. You may still be very emotionally connected to him, and even though you are no longer willing to be his partner in deceit and know your emotional survival depends on ending the relationship, he'll most likely pull out every stop in an attempt to keep you hooked in.

Sometimes, as in my friend Diana's case, a sociopath will make it a little easier for you and disappear. But most of the time he's going to attach himself to you like a barnacle, and you'll have your work cut out for you.

At no time is it more important than when you're ending a relationship with this type of man to be clear and concise in your communication. He must take you seriously, and you must avoid any mixed messages that might encourage him to think you're still vulnerable to his manipulation. You need to tell him in no uncertain terms that the relationship is over. Say things like:

- "I've given this a lot of thought, and I've decided that this relationship is not working for me. I've decided to end it."
- "Please don't make any attempts to contact me. Don't call, don't write, don't come over."
- "I'm sorry, but this is not negotiable, and I don't want to talk about it any further."

I know these phrases sound cold, but they are designed to protect you from a further onslaught of his pleas, excuses, and promises. Don't fall into the trap of giving "good reasons" or long explanations if he continues to pressure you. And by all means avoid the impulse to tell him what a bastard he's been, as tempting as that may be. Explaining yourself or telling him off only serves to open the door for him to argue with you and show you why you're wrong about him.

As with all new behavior, rehearse, rehearse, rehearse. Practice saying these lines until they become comfortable for you. You are not being cruel, you are being appropriately assertive. Besides, when was the last time he worried about being cruel to you?

GIVING YOURSELF GOOD ADVICE

Laurie, the sculptor who had been on an emotional roller coaster for a year and a half with Michael, the marriage and family counselor who had sexually exploited several of his clients, knew that the time had come for her to get out of the madness. But when she told Michael her decision, he used every trick in his repertoire to persuade her to give him another chance:

I was really determined. I know how close I came to ending up in the funny farm with this guy. So I called him at his office, and when he called back, I told him it was over. He cried. He swore he realized how much he'd hurt me. He says he'll go into therapy. He says he's through with Karen, that it's only me, and I can't abandon him now—

I interrupted her. "Laurie," I said, "I can finish the speech for you. I know what he said because it's the same speech that just about every woman who's ever been involved with a man like this has heard. You've grown a lot in the past few months, and I think you're ready to give yourself the answers you need instead of my giving them to you. So let's switch roles. You're the therapist, and I'm in your place. What would you say to me?

Susan (as Laurie): He's being so pathetic, I can't bear it. How can I hurt him like this?

Laurie (as Susan): This is his grand finale, his ultimate performance piece. Remember, he's not capable of real feelings. His tears, his misery, are just as superficial and contrived as all the other acts he's put on for you. And as far as his promises are concerned, count up the times he's made the same promises to you and broken them within the week.

Susan (as Laurie): But what if he threatens to kill himself?

Laurie (as Susan): I wouldn't worry about that too much. Depressed people kill themselves. Narcissistic assholes rarely do.

Susan: Hey, not bad. If you ever get tired of being a sculptor, you can always become a therapist.

By stepping out of her own shoes for a few moments, Laurie immediately became more objective about Michael. She was able to reinforce what she had learned by putting her insights into words. As a result, she was able to return to doing what she needed to do.

If you find yourself wavering in the face of his efforts to make you feel sorry for him and change your mind, or because your feelings are tripping you up, use the exercise I did with Laurie and tell yourself the same sorts of things Laurie said about Michael. It also helps to imagine that someone you care deeply about—a daughter or a beloved friend—is involved with a man like this and you can see him far more objectively than she can. What would you say to her if she weakened in her resolve? Putting your knowledge about him into words is a powerful reality check.

By the way, to show you how sincere Michael's grief was about losing Laurie, a few days after she broke off with him, he moved back in with his wife, Karen.

In addition to the practical considerations of ending the relationship, you're going to have a lot of other practical matters to deal with, such as trying to recoup money he's taken from you, finding competent legal and financial counsel if you were married to him or mixed your money with his, and protecting yourself from him in the future.

PROTECTING YOURSELF

Sociopaths are volatile and unpredictable. A man like this is extremely self-absorbed, and you're doing something that shows him he's no longer in control and that makes him look bad. The one genuine emotion sociopaths experience is rage, especially when they're thwarted. Therefore, when you're ending the relationship, I want you to err on the side of caution.

If he's explosive, you've probably had indications during the time you've been with him. But nobody has a crystal ball, and as I advise women who are leaving nonsociopathic men, even a man who may have shown no tendencies toward violence may lose it at this time. There are ways of letting him know the relationship is over without putting yourself in danger. You can let him know in a public place such as a restaurant, or by phone, as Laurie did, or letter. There's nothing that says you have to do it face-to-face.

If you're living with him and need to get your things out, take someone with you, preferably a male friend or relative. If you need to get him out of your place, tell him to leave when you have someone there to protect you. If he refuses, get out, call the police, and explain the situation to them. There are trespassing laws that can be enforced under these circumstances. Don't be afraid to use every means at your disposal to show him you mean business. That includes restraining orders, pressing charges, and all the other unpleasant things many women have to do when they break up with a volatile man. Under no circumstances be alone with him when you give him the news.

Right now, I know some of you are thinking, "He would never hurt me" or "He would never do anything like that"—and you might be right. But why take a chance? I know some of you may also think I'm being melodramatic or overly cautious, but all you have to do is read the daily paper or watch television to see how dangerous your situation is. This man is not a nice, normal neurotic—he's much more disturbed. This is no time to bury your head in the sand.

How Could This Happen to Me?

You've now put the sociopath out of your life, but he's not out of your thoughts. With the emerging recognition of what has happened to you comes a truckload of shame and humiliation. Having finally recognized the sociopath for what he is, you are probably having a profound crisis of confidence in yourself and your judgment. You may believe that there must be something very wrong with you and that your judgment about human nature must be hopelessly flawed.

Ruth, the entertainment lawyer, had just such a failure of confidence once she realized that her marriage could not continue. Ruth had quit therapy against my advice once she was convinced that she and her husband, Craig, had entered a new phase of their marriage. Unfortunately, this honeymoon period only lasted a few months. Then Craig's powerful compulsion to bed half the female population of Los Angeles took over once again. Ruth called and made an appointment to see me. It was a very subdued and depressed Ruth who walked in a few days later. She spoke slowly as she shredded her already very wet Kleenex:

I wouldn't blame you if you said, "I told you so." How could I think he would change when he's been doing the same thing for years? I even made you out to be my enemy because you were so skeptical. God, Susan, I'm an intelligent woman—I meet men like this in my practice all the time. I just wouldn't believe it could happen to me. At any rate, I found out about another one—a young actress client of his—and I've already filed for divorce. I just feel so stupid. . . ."

I told Ruth that I had no intention of saying "I told you so." In fact, this was one of those times where there was very little satisfaction in being right. But with a man like Craig, it's pretty easy to predict what will happen. It was also pretty easy to predict that Ruth would be doing a lot of beating up on herself.

SELF-FLAGELLATION

One of the sad ironies for many women in the aftermath of a relationship with a sociopath is that they are very often more angry at themselves than they are at the man who has so badly manipulated and deceived them.

No matter how crazy your relationship may have been, there will still be an inevitable sense that you must have done something wrong. No longer able or willing to deny, rationalize, or cover up, you bombard yourself with thoughts like:

- How could I have been so blind?
- How could I have been so stupid?
- How could I have let him use me like that?
- How could I have stayed with him so long?
- How could I have ignored all the warning signs?

Most women go through this kind of self-flagellation after any kind of breakup, and a breakup with a sociopath really brings out the self-reproach demons with a vengeance. But these questions, as painful as they may be, are actually a form of recognition. They are actually good! They are part of your wake-up call. Welcome them. They are a sure sign that your eyes are now fully open and your ability to respond with appropriate emotion is intact. They are a sign that you are no longer the woman who accepted the abnormal and convinced yourself that it was just fine. Pat yourself on the back for getting out!

BEING DECEIVED DOESN'T MEAN BEING STUPID

Once again you can accelerate your healing by stepping out of your own situation and imagining you are comforting someone you care about who has just gone through a breakup with a sociopath. As your daughter or sister or friend, say all the self-reproachful things you have been saying to yourself. Now, as the voice of comfort and wisdom, answer her out loud. Ruth chose to do this exercise by imagining her sister Laura, with whom she'd always been very close, sitting in the empty chair after ending her marriage. Here are some of things she said to her:

"Honey, I know you feel awful right now, but you were just looking for love in the wrong place. He looked so good on the surface, it's no wonder you were drawn to him. He's a real pro! And you can't beat yourself up for being loyal and not wanting to give up on him. And don't you dare call yourself stupid— you're one of the smartest people I know! He's just so persuasive and glib. I don't know who would have had the awareness to know it was all bullshit. But you know now, and you've done something about it. You're so brave and so strong. I really take my hat off to you."

"Wow!" exclaimed Ruth. "Where did that come from?"

"It came," I answered, "from that very special place inside you—your spark or your spirit or your light or whatever you want to call it. The place that no one can harm no matter how deeply you've been wounded. That's where we go to heal. And there is forgiveness needed. Not for him, but for you. You really need to forgive yourself."

Ruth was quiet for a few seconds. Then she said, "I guess my job is to start being as nice to myself as I would be to someone else in my situation."

It is always a revelation when we see clearly how hard we are being on ourselves and how much more loving we instinctively are to someone else. This is true for most women, not just those who have been involved with sociopaths. Remind yourself regularly that you did the best you could with the level of awareness you had. Sociopaths are very slick and persuasive. By the time you realize something's very wrong, you may be deeply involved with him. So give yourself a break. It's time to start being as good a friend to yourself as you are to others. Maybe that could be the new golden rule.

EVERY ENDING BRINGS SADNESS

It would be wonderful if every woman who has lived with the chaos and betrayal of a liar could wake up one morning, immediately feel better, and cut off her sadness and sense of loss.

It's easy for other people to say, "Just get on with your life— you're so much better off without him." And, of course, you are. But any breakup, whether with a man as destructive as a sociopath or one with good qualities, feels as if the emotional rug has been pulled out from under you, leaving behind a sense of loss and even mourning. There will certainly be times when you miss him. Don't be ashamed to admit that to yourself. Despite all the insanity, there were undoubtedly many good times.

Once you have reached the point of truly knowing that the only way you have a chance at the kind of relationship—not to mention the kind of life—you deserve is to leave the man who has deceived you, you will find the courage to hold tight to what you know and to stay on the path that will lead you there. Your integrity and emotional well-being are at stake. Those are precious commodities, and protecting them by staying true to your decision is the most life-affirming thing you can do for yourself.

12

Learning to Trust Again

No matter which path you have chosen—whether you're working to put your relationship back on track or struggling to regain your balance as you move forward without your partner—I know how shaky and vulnerable you feel. The wounds of betrayal and deception cut deep. But being wounded is not the end of your journey—it's the beginning. It's what you do with your wounds that will determine the quality of the rest of your life.

In your postbetrayal universe, part of you may be tempted to lock your hurt away behind a new kind of armor, a harsher view of life and love that's more skeptical, more guarded. "Never again!" you say. You've promised yourself that you will do everything necessary to guard your battered heart, even if that means retreating into isolation, or building such an impenetrable wall around yourself that no one can get through.

But the work that you've done so far has changed you forever. It has reintroduced you to a woman who has been able to face a painful situation with courage, and live with intense and difficult emotions without crumbling.

Please don't underestimate the tremendous resources you've called up from deep within yourself to move through the crisis of betrayal. The process of healing involves making the continuing choice to find and use the best parts of yourself. True healing comes when you can see your emotional scars as a proof of your strengths rather than as a badge of vulnerability. As you become more and more able to do that, you'll come to some very exciting discoveries: Whether you stay or leave, you can risk opening yourself up again when you're ready, and even risk being deceived again, because now you have survival skills you didn't have before. That means you don't have to wear armor for protection. Instead, you can tap the wisdom that resides in your wounds.

THE FIRST STEP IS TRUST

If you step outside yourself and look back at the experience you've had as though it were the plot of a novel, what do you see? When I ask that question of women who have struggled with lying in their relationships, the answers I hear reveal a great deal about how harshly we tend to judge ourselves.

Allison answered like this:

If you want to know the truth, I see a too-trusting woman who was willing to believe everything her husband told her because she couldn't even imagine that he was cheating. I just didn't get it. I was so damned naive.

Kathy said:

I see a woman who went against almost everything she believed in. She stopped trusting her judgment. She blamed herself for her husband's lies. She didn't insist that he take personal responsibility. She kept rescuing him and covering for him. It was as if she lost herself for a time.

It's very normal to tell yourself that your pain was punishment for bad judgment—for being too trusting. The emotional scars look like convincing evidence that you were a fool to trust, to make yourself vulnerable, to believe in your lover's promises to keep you safe and loved. But as I'll show you, that's a serious misreading of what it means to be wounded, and it's based on a misunderstanding of what trust is and where it really comes from.

A NEW DEFINITION OF TRUST

For most of us, trust has been a quality that's completely dependent on the other person. We've offered it, then waited to see if
we were right. Trust was a game of chance, or a step onto a div-
ing board above a pool that might or might not be filled. No wonder it feels so precarious to consider trusting again.

Anne found herself struggling with just such a bitter legacy,
even though Randy was obviously sincere in his desire to rebuild
their marriage:

*I trusted him so much, and he destroyed that. I honestly don't
know if I can ever get that back. I want to trust him, and he's
really doing everything I asked of him, but I'm so confused. And
I'm so afraid of being hurt again—I don't know if I could stand it.*

It's understandable that Anne had the impulse to retrench as
she sifted through the ashes of what she once believed in. "Pull
back," she told herself. "Lower your expectations." And above all,
"Don't get hurt again."

Innocent, unquestioning love is a casualty of betrayal, and like
Anne, when we realize it's gone, we don't know what to replace it
with. You may have decided that once intimacy has been violated,
it can never be truly regained. You doubt men, you doubt yourself,
and you are struggling as never before with the issue of trust.

But what if from here on out you decided to look at trust as
something that is not a tentative, fearful venture toward another
person but rather a safe, clear path that leads you home, to the
strength in yourself. What if you were to change your idea of
trust from something to be given away to something that resides
in you? What if you stopped worrying so much about trusting the
other person and instead focused on trusting yourself?

LEARNING TO TRUST YOURSELF

"I'm not sure I know what you mean," said Anne. "As far as I
know, I do trust myself—I'm honest, I'm competent, I'm a good
mom, I manage well in the world."

"And that's great stuff to know about yourself," I told her, "but I want you to consider one other facet of trust—the kind we worry about in love relationships. The kind of trust I'm talking about is where you can say, 'I trust my judgment, I trust my courage to confront lying if and when I encounter it again, and most of all, I trust myself to be able to handle whatever life throws at me.' You can't take all your trust and just hand it over to someone else for safekeeping. Randy needs to earn back your trust in him, and I hope he does. But don't give it all away.

"You need to hang on to a lot of trust for yourself. That means that you continue to build your emotional and intellectual resources so that the time will come when you can truly know: 'If I'm hurt again, I can stand it. I will deal with it, and ultimately I will get over it.' Once you believe that, you can open your heart again knowing that you'll be OK no matter what. That's the kind of trust you can always count on."

A few weeks later Anne reported a wonderful shift in how she was feeling:

You know, it's amazing what happened when I stopped focusing so much on him and started calming myself. I take at least a half hour each day just to sit quietly and think about the strengths I have and how much love I have in my life—not only from Randy but from my child, my family, my friends. I must be a pretty terrific person to have all those wonderful people caring so much about me. So that's something I can trust as well. And I'm really starting to understand what you mean about self-trust. Let's say, worst case scenario, things don't work out with Randy. I think they will, but no matter what, I know I'll survive and I know how to love. I'll make it.

At last report, things were working out well for Anne and Randy. The one thing I can count on for sure is that Anne now knows the real meaning of trust.

TUNING IN TO WHAT YOU KNOW

Once you realize that trust is an inside job and that the person holding the safety net is you, you may feel a little unsteady until you see all the resources you have for building trust in yourself. For instance, there's the early warning system that was giving you clues that something was amiss in your relationship. An important part of learning to trust yourself is to recognize that you probably knew much more than you were willing to admit to yourself.

We women are very perceptive creatures. Intuition seems to be almost encoded in our genetic structure. Feelings and hunches reveal themselves to us in the form of that wise inner voice that usually tells us what we need to know. Unfortunately, many of us brush away what that voice is telling us because many times it's not what we want to hear.

Toward the end of my work with Carol, she said something that most of us can relate to:

Looking back, I realize I knew everything I needed to know about Ken after the first two weeks. I just didn't pay attention.

As you reflect on your experience with lying, you, too, may be able to see that something inside you was telling you troubling things about your partner's behavior, but you chose to turn down the volume and not listen. Instead you embraced denial and rationalization because they were more comfortable—and, of course, they let you down.

Now, because of what you've been through, you have the ability to tune in to what you know and to trust your perceptions. When that inner voice says, "Something's wrong," pay attention. It always tells you the truth.

That doesn't mean you're going to get it perfect every time—nobody does. There will be times, either with the man you're staying with or a new man, when you'll be too suspicious or you'll overreact. And there will be times when you're too accepting and overlook some real red flags. But you're not going to do any of those things as often as you used to, and you're much more able now to step back and evaluate what's going on based on a new willingness to listen to what your inner voice is telling you.

TIME OUT

If you have decided to end your relationship, you also need to take time away from the inevitable distractions that are built into romance and family life. Time for yourself to process this new wisdom is an essential part of your healing—don't be afraid to take it. You may believe that the best way to try to ease the pain of a breakup is to jump into another intimate relationship right way. Don't. Dating is fine, but give yourself time—lots of time— before you get hot and heavy with anyone again.

The old clichés about how love on the rebound will take you from the frying pan into the fire are clichés because they contain an element of truth. You need time to fully explore and process what happened to you and to develop a solid trust in yourself. You may get involved with somebody in order to avoid doing those things because it seems like too much work, rather than because you're ready to build a new relationship. You may very well want to lose yourself in romance, or believe that the attention from a new man would do a world of good for your confidence and bruised self-respect. But what you really need more than anything else right now is a sense of wholeness—and that involves looking into yourself.

AVOIDING A REPEAT PERFORMANCE . . .

But of course the time will come when you will want to connect with a new lover. Women who are looking toward new relationships often worry that they'll somehow be magnetically drawn to another man who lies and find themselves repeating the whole nightmare again. Jan wanted a guarantee that she wouldn't do just that:

What I'd really like, of course, is some kind of internal Geiger counter or alarm system that would rattle, hum, and screech at the first breath of a lie from someone I'm attracted to. But I know there's no such device, and since I can't attach a lie detector to every guy I start seeing, I'm not sure what to do.

I told Jan that of course there are no guarantees, because a lot of men who lie are very persuasive and skillful. But as she began to move into new relationships, she could begin to pay special attention to a set of warning signs that she had glossed over in the past.

As you get to know a new man, ask yourself the following questions. They may not sound terribly romantic, but as you know now, there's nothing romantic about being deceived.

- Are there inconsistencies in what he tells you about his history, his work, his financial situation, and other aspects of his life?
- Has he acknowledged that he's been unfaithful in the past but "now it's different"?
- If you press him for information about something that concerns you, does he accuse you of being too possessive or suspicious?
- Is he evasive about giving clear answers about his current involvements with other women or his living situation?
- If you've caught him in a lie already, how has he responded? Did he deny he lied, or did he acknowledge it and take responsibility for his behavior? Does his explanation for why he lied sound plausible?

These questions can be an emotional life insurance policy for you. They will help tell you the truth about lying. And they'll go a long way toward lowering your tolerance for lies.

MYTHS AND MISCONCEPTIONS

You'll notice that nowhere on this list do you see any of the old wives' tales about how to spot a liar through body language. How many times have you heard, for example, that you can tell someone's lying if he won't look you straight in the eye? Well, I've got news for you. Eye contact and facial expressions are very easy to control. Some liars, especially the more practiced ones, will calmly look you in the eye and tell you that the sun comes up in the West. Conversely, another man who's telling the truth may avoid direct eye contact because of his particular personality traits. He may, for example, be shy, feel nervous, or have some-thing distracting going on in his life at the time.

Other long-believed but totally unreliable indicators of lying include:

- Voice pitch
- Too much smiling
- Fidgeting or restlessness
- Flushing, perspiring, or fast breathing

Despite what you may have believed for years, many liars—especially those who are comfortable with deception or who have come to believe their own lies—won't exhibit any of these signs.

As you become more aware of the real warning signs, you'll see that men who lie reveal themselves fairly early. They're more evasive than open; they don't like answering questions about themselves directly; they offer vague or implausible explanations to your questions.

DEVELOPING A LOW TOLERANCE FOR LYING

In the past, you may have let the strong currents of attraction carry you right past concerns about a man's behavior. But with your new awareness of the costs and consequences of lying, you can slow down and look at a new relationship more carefully.

You may be disappointed to find that a man you're attracted to is not the open person you hoped he'd be. But as you now know, it's far better to find that out sooner than later. And for heaven's sake, don't beat yourself up because you found yourself attracted to another liar, as Jan did:

"Do I have a sign on my forehead?? Honest to god, I think I'm cursed! I met this gorgeous guy at a party, and after seeing him for about two weeks I knew he was full of crap about almost everything. He told me he'd been divorced for two years, and a mutual friend told me his divorce isn't final and that they're a long way from a settlement. It's depressing as hell!"

"Bravo," I said.

"What do you mean, bravo?" asked a bewildered Jan.

"Maybe as soon as you get done whipping yourself with birch branches, you can notice all the things you've done differently."

Jan thought for a long moment and then said:

"Well . . . I knew very early that he was lying about a major fact of his life. I also told him what I'd found out and gave him a chance to explain. But all he did was talk about what a disloyal bitch the friend who told me about him was. Then I told him I didn't want to see him again. Yeah—I guess that's pretty different . . . . Oh, well— on to the next one."

It's no reflection on your character, intelligence, luck, or ability to choose men wisely if you are attracted to a man who falls into the negative patterns you are now so familiar with. We can't know everything about a person immediately, and many men who lie are extremely convincing and charming in the beginning. Being attracted to a liar is no sign of regression. The crucial indicator of the change in you is what you choose to do about it. If, like Jan, you face the lies head-on without denial, rationalizations, or blind acceptance, then you can know you've lost your tolerance for lying.

THE HEALING POWER OF WOMEN'S FRIENDSHIPS

So far we have focused almost entirely on relationships with men. But there is a vast treasure available to all of us that too many women overlook in their quest for the "great romance." It is the understanding and support we can find in the friendship of women. Remember when I talked about the five "C's" that would lead you to healing? This is the heart of the fifth C: connecting with friends.

These friendships are not a stopgap to fill time between relationships with men. Even if you are staying with your lover or have become involved with a new one, you still need the unique comfort and encouragement that women friends can give you. You may have been so preoccupied with the problems in your relationship that you neglected or pulled away from your friends, claiming you didn't have time for them. Work, children, a troubled marriage, or a love affair can swallow us up, and often we put our women friends at the bottom of our list of priorities. But it's amazing to see what happens when we give them their rightful place at the top.

Diane acknowledged that she had put her friendships on hold and wondered if it was too late to do something about it:

I've been so overwhelmed with just staying afloat that I've really lost touch with my friends. There are two women in particular that I really miss, and I've made no effort to see them. God, I'd feel so guilty calling and saying "Hey! I'm a wreck. I just split with Ben and I need some shoring up."

"Do it," I said. "What's the worst thing that can happen? Even if you can't reconnect with them, you'll be no worse off than you are now. But I'll bet if you tell them the truth about what's been going on and how sorry you are to have let them drop out of your life, they'll probably be delighted to get together with you. You need women friends now, Diane. In fact, there's no time in our lives when we don't need them—even if we're in a wonderful relationship."

Yes, it's awkward to call someone after a long silence, but most women find that their friends are happy to welcome them back. When we disappear from someone who's been close, we forget that they miss us too.

Women's friendships are like the handwork women have done for centuries. Elegant and strong, lovingly crafted, they build with the attention we give them. Most of them can also withstand being put aside, sometimes for long periods, and taken up again when we're ready.

We reconnect with women we care about, and it's as though we can almost always find our way to where the conversation ended, pick up the thread, and continue. Our women friends can be a vital part of our memory, reminding us of parts of ourselves we've forgotten, disasters we've survived, impossible dreams we've seen into being. They are also the accepting ears who will hear our story as we try to make sense of it, and help us puzzle out what we want next.

In many cultures around the world, women gather to mark the significant passages of their lives—marriage, the birth of children, the beginning and ending of fertility, the death of loved ones. In their stories, their sharing of experience, they guide and help ease the transition from one phase of life to another. Over time, the story of one person's difficulty or suffering becomes a part of the knowledge of the group and builds every member's ability to deal with adversity. We endure more easily knowing that others have. And we appreciate our own resilience more fully as our stories are told and received with love and compassion.

Bringing this kind of sharing into your own life doesn't require any special kind of ritual or shaman. It requires only that you actively maintain friendships with women.

Diane not only reconnected with her two old friends, but they brought her into a book discussion club they were part of, which provided some rewarding social and intellectual stimulation for her. It was the beginning of her reentry into a sane, and safer world. She was finding her wise heart.

THE WISE HEART

At first glance, those words may seem to be in direct conflict with each other. After all, wisdom resides in the mind, and the heart is the seat of emotions, so what on earth is a wise heart?

For me, a wise heart is the wisdom that comes from the delicate balance of intellect and emotion—the ability to think and feel at the same time. When we listen to our inner voice, we are using intuition and feeling to guide us. When we ask ourselves the questions on the various lists in this chapter and others, we are switching into the reasoning, observing part of our being. Both are equally important. That's the balance we all strive for. If one of those components dominates the other, we get into trouble. Running on pure emotion obscures our ability to see things clearly or rationally and may propel us into impulsive, self-defeating behavior. But if we shut down our feelings and only trust our intellect, we cheat ourselves out of experiencing the richness of our feelings. We are not truly alive.

A wise heart flourishes not tentatively but with all the determination and courage of a woman who has decided that her pain will not turn to bitterness and that loss can be a beginning, not an end. It chooses to risk loving because its natural impulse is to open, not close.

FROM WOUNDS TO WISDOM

The wise heart knows that being wounded by a lover's deception and betrayal does not mean that you are permanently impaired or damaged. Your wounds are evidence only that you are human, you have feelings, and you've been hurt. In fact, the wounds of betrayal and deception can be a great source of information and wisdom—if you take the courageous and comforting step of listening to them.

The depth and details of all your experiences are there: where you made mistakes, what hurts you, what you can live with, and what's intolerable. Your wounds know what danger feels like, and they resonate now with a new sensitivity.

As you continue to grow in courage and strength, you will learn how to transform the wounds of betrayal and deception into the wisdom that will illuminate your path. As you enter this new phase of your life, your wounds will inform you, protect you, and provide an endless stream of valuable information in the steady pulse of the wise heart.

MOVING TOWARD WHOLENESS

A few months after Diane finished therapy with me, I got this letter from her:

> *Dear Susan:*
> *Over the weekend I was in the mountains hiking with some friends. We were going up a steep hill, and I was doing fine until I turned a corner and saw a huge boulder in my path. I looked at it for a long time and got scared. Finally I realized I could see some places to wedge in my feet. I took a deep breath and started climbing. I was a lot slower than the people I was with, but I told them to go on ahead—I'd catch up. When I got to the top of that rock, I had a view of the most beautiful valley I'd ever seen. And I was so proud of myself for making the effort to find a way to get there instead of just giving up. I loved the feeling of being on that solid rock. I knew it wasn't going to*

crumble under me, and I was on top of the world.

When I got home, I realized that that climb was a great metaphor for my life. During all the ups and downs with Ben, I really felt powerless a lot of the time. I felt like there was quicksand all around me, and I never knew what was going to pull me down next. You know what a mess I was when I found out what was really going on. I seriously didn't think I could go on. All I could see was a huge boulder blocking my way, and I never thought I had the strength in me to try to keep going. But you reminded me of all the brains and heart and real stubbornness I have—and I made myself put one foot in front of the other, day by day.

I know you told me often that if I kept demanding honesty and stayed honest with myself, my life would change. I look around me now and I finally know, deep in my bones, what you meant. Look at me! I'm hiking with friends. I'm doing volunteer work for the first time in years. And I'm meeting men who seem interesting. I'm not afraid to spend time finding out what they're really like, and believe me, I know when they've got the lying gene. I also know that I don't have to let liars into my life, ever again. I'm building my life on rock, Susan. I'm sad for what's gone from my life, but I've been through so much that I know I can handle anything now. Even taking a chance on love.

Love from the other
side of the mountain,
Diane

Diane was not the same person who walked into her relationship, and neither are you. Every step you take to remain open to life and love after a betrayal or a loss of trust moves you toward wisdom. The wise heart chooses not to hold onto the pain of the past, but to go on. It remembers and honors the person you have become—a woman who has gathered the skills to move, day by day, toward her own wholeness.

ACKNOWLEDGMENTS

There are many people whose support and encouragement helped make this book happen:

My collaborator Donna Frazier whose patience and dedication never fail and who skillfully helped tell this story.

My wonderful agent Virginia Barber and all the great people who work with her, especially Jennifer Rudolph Walsh and Jay Mandel for their fervent belief in me and my work.

My editor Joëlle Delbourgo for her never-ending pursuit of excellence and her warm encouragement.

My family and friends for their love and wisdom.

To my clients, friends, and relatives who generously shared their stories and who are the heart of this book.

And most of all, for my wonderful daughter Wendy, who has taught me so much and gives me so much joy.

SUSAN FORWARD maintains offices in Los Angeles, California.
For further information, call (818) 986-1161.

Books by internationally acclaimed therapist

SUSAN FORWARD, Ph.D.

EMOTIONAL BLACKMAIL
(with Donna Frazier)

Emotional blackmail—a powerful form of manipulation in which people close to us threaten to punish us for not doing what they want. Whether they are parents or partners, bosses or coworkers, friends or lovers, emotional blackmailers know our vulnerabilities and deepest secrets, and use this intimate knowledge to gain our eventual compliance. Now in this helpful book, Susan Forward gives blackmail victims the invaluable tools they need to fight back and strengthen their relationships.

"A helpful book . . . [it] makes a whole lot of sense for the person who feels controlled by someone else's needs, whines, and threats."
—*Detroit News/Free Press*

ISBN 0-06-092897-2 (trade paperback)
ISBN 0-694-51837-9 (audiocassette)

WHEN YOUR LOVER IS A LIAR
(with Donna Frazier)

A powerful book that provides sound advice for women whose men betray their confidence, *When Your Lover Is a Liar* shows how to survive and thrive despite deception in relationships. Forward expertly profiles the wide variety of liars, tells how to deal with lies from the benign to the lethal, gives practical strategies to stop them before they ruin your relationship and your life, and shows the path to rebuilding respect and trust in yourself and your partner.

"An outstanding guide for helping women reduce the trauma of . . . interpersonal violations, choose a direction, and rebuild their sense of self."
—Janis Abrams Spring, Ph.D., author of *After the Affair*

ISBN 0-06-093115-9 (trade paperback)
ISBN 0-694-52111-6 (audiocassette)

Available at bookstores everywhere, or call 1-800-331-3761 to order.